Fashion Buying

Second Edition

Helen Goworek
Senior Lecturer, Nottingham Trent University

Blackwell
Publishing

Blackwell Publishing editorial offices:
Blackwell Publishing Ltd, 9600 Garsington Road, Oxford OX4 2DQ, UK
Tel: +44 (0)1865 776868
Blackwell Publishing Professional, 2121 State Avenue, Ames, Iowa 50014-8300, USA
Tel: +1 515 292 0140
Blackwell Publishing Asia Pty Ltd, 550 Swanston Street, Carlton, Victoria 3053, Australia
Tel: +61 (0)3 8359 1011

First edition published 2001 by Blackwell Science, a Blackwell Publishing company
Second edition published 2007 by Blackwell Publishing Ltd

ISBN: 9781405149921

Library of Congress Cataloging-in-Publication Data

Goworek, Helen.
Fashion buying / Helen Goworek. – 2nd ed.
p. cm.
Includes bibliographical references and index.
ISBN-13: 978-1-4051-4992-1 (pbk. : alk. paper)
ISBN-10: 1-4051-4992-2 (pbk. : alk. paper) 1. Fashion merchandising–Vocational guidance. 2. Purchasing–Vocational guidance. 3. Clothing trade–Vocational guidance. I. Title.

HD9940.A2G68 2007
391.0068′7–dc22 2006101282

A catalogue record for this title is available from the British Library

Set in 10/12.5 pt Optima
by Graphicraft Limited, Hong Kong
Printed and bound in Singapore
by COS Printers Pte Ltd

The publisher's policy is to use permanent paper from mills that operate a sustainable forestry policy, and which has been manufactured from pulp processed using acid-free and elementary chlorine-free practices. Furthermore, the publisher ensures that the text paper and cover board used have met acceptable environmental accreditation standards.

For further information on Blackwell Publishing, visit our website:
www.blackwellpublishing.com

Contents

Acknowledgements

Many people have supported me in writing this book, either by being interviewed or by reading relevant chapters and making useful recommendations. I would like to thank the following people (in alphabetical order), all of whom have influenced the content of this book: Winifred Aldrich, Nick Atkinson, Suzi Avens, Alison Beattie, Johnnie Boden, Sandra Bojko, Steve Cochrane, Anya Coote, Amy Davis, Vanessa Denza, Christine Gerrard, Andrew Grimes, Rachel Hollis, Corri Homan-Berry, Louise Housley, Tracey Jacob, Beth Jelly, Zarina Kanji, Ruth Kelly, Vrjay Krishnan, Pete Mellor, Safia Minney, Jo Mould, Rachel Neame, Moriamo Oshodi, Neil Prosser, Julia Richards, Kathy Salisbury, Marisa Shutt, Ruth Spinks, Joyce Thornton, Debbie Torr, Kate Wells. The late Richard Miles was responsible for giving me the opportunity to fulfil a long-held ambition by commissioning the original version of this book. I would like to thank my tutors from the BA (Hons) Fashion Marketing degree at Newcastle Polytechnic (now the University of Northumbria), Vivien Todd, and the late Liz Ford, who encouraged and inspired me to work within the fashion industry and to become involved in fashion design education.

Preface

This book explains the responsibilities of the fashion buyer. It is based partly on my own experience and on interviews undertaken during 2006 with buyers working for six different fashion companies, from assistant to managerial level, thereby offering a broad and current perspective on the buying function. Buying can be a lucrative career at all levels of the fashion market, as a wide range of skills is required to fulfil this demanding role. Buying fashion merchandise differs significantly from buying for other product types, owing to the relatively short life cycle of fashion items, the majority of which become obsolete within six months. It is this planned obsolescence which simultaneously boosts sales within the clothing industry through the constant introduction of new products, and constantly challenges buyers and designers to develop innovative and profitable clothing ranges.

At the start of my career in the fashion industry as a trainee buyer, I found myself exposed to new systems and a language with which I was unfamiliar. Having secured this post shortly after graduation, I had no real idea of what the job would entail apart from a perception that I would be responsible for a large amount of the company's money by selecting clothes intended to appeal to target customers. At the time, I did not realise that it usually takes some years before a buyer is given this level of responsibility. I wondered why no 'guide to buying' was available to explain the relevant terminology and procedures, as this would have been very helpful to me and my colleagues. The aim of this book, therefore, is to document the information which I would have found useful before embarking on a career in buying. The book also aims to inform those in the field of fashion design about the role of the buyers with whom they regularly work.

The content of the book has been completely revised for the second edition, though the format remains the same. Several chapters contain additional information, to reflect the substantial changes that have occurred since the publication of the first edition, namely the impact of the internet, increasing import penetration and the consequent demise of clothing manufacture in the UK. All of the case studies are new or updated, with only one of the interviewees remaining in the same post since the 2001 edition.

Chapter 1

Introduction

This book focuses on the buying of fashion merchandise, particularly clothing, but the processes involved apply also to a broader range of merchandise, such as footwear and accessories, since all of these products contribute to creating a total image for the consumer in response to changing trends. The clothing market is a significant sector of the UK economy, with total sales worth £35.6 billion in 2005 (Retail Intelligence, 2006). The outlook for fashion buying jobs is positive, as sales volume in the UK fashion market is forecast to increase steadily until at least 2010 (Key Note, 2006), and buyers play a central role in the development and commercial success of products within this market. Fashion buyers are versatile individuals, combining interpersonal and organisational skills with a knowledge of products and processes. Fashion buying is a challenging role requiring stamina and enthusiasm in order to succeed.

What do fashion buyers do?

This question is answered in some depth within this book. There can be no standard job description for a buyer as the role and title vary between companies. In short, all fashion buyers are responsible for selecting a range of products aimed at a specific market for a specific company, for example, mass market girls' leisurewear or middle market lingerie. Some of the tasks undertaken by buyers in order to select a range successfully include:

- identifying relevant fashion trends
- liaising with suppliers of products
- presenting ranges of selected merchandise to colleagues and management
- calculating profit margins
- monitoring and analysing the sales performance of fashion ranges
- reviewing and analysing competitors' ranges.

It is essential that the buyer is familiar with the type of customers at whom the company's products are targeted as the aim of buying the range is to sell the goods profitably. Most buyers start their careers as an assistant or trainee, working in a supportive role for a buyer before being given the responsibility of the tasks listed above. As every retailer operates differently most of a buyer's training is hands-on, and involves shadowing and helping an experienced buyer. There are various levels of responsibility for buyers, often dependent upon the size of the retailer. Buying teams are normally headed by buying managers or directors who manage staff, coordinate buying and promotional strategies with other senior managers, and have a full overview of the ranges within their remit.

Chapters 8, 9 and 10 contain case studies of buyers, with different levels of responsibility, from various UK fashion retailers to give the reader a realistic and current perspective on this important job. No two days are alike for a fashion buyer and activities can vary from inputting data on new styles into a computer to visiting fashion stores in Milan. Administrative duties undoubtedly outnumber those aspects of the role which are perceived as glamorous, which reflects the immense amount of background work which goes into buying fashion products, most of which remains unseen by the consumer. Buyers cannot function in isolation so buying a fashion range is always the result of teamwork, and the buyer is constantly reliant on other departments within the company as well as on an external network of suppliers. The role of the fashion buyer is constantly developing to reflect changes in consumer tastes and the introduction of technology.

During the six years since the first edition of this book was published, rapid and significant changes in the way the fashion industry operates have impacted on the role of the fashion buyer: the market has become almost saturated by imported merchandise and the internet is developing into a major method of distribution for fashion products. The volatile nature of the fashion business has meant that during this period many fashion retailers have expanded or changed ownership whilst others have been edged out of the market. This second edition aims to reflect these changes in relation to the job of the fashion buyer.

Fashion market levels

Mass market fashion chainstores dominate the UK high street, so by far the majority of fashion buying jobs are within this sector. The owners of smaller independent stores which sell middle-market and designer labels often take on the responsibility of the buying role themselves, or they may employ buyers who have other duties within the store. A significantly higher proportion of womenswear is sold than menswear in the UK, with menswear accounting for only one-third of the total value of the clothing and footwear market (Retail Intelligence, 1999). As a result there are more womenswear fashion retailers, and therefore more womenswear fashion buyers, than there are menswear or childrenswear fashion buyers. However there is more competition for womenswear buying jobs and specialising in either menswear or childrenswear can be a good career move. The two main methods of buying fashion products are:

- developing products which are exclusive to a particular retailer or mail order company (sometimes referred to as 'own label')
- buying branded fashion merchandise.

The former applies to retail fashion multiples and mail order companies, and the cost of overheads for product development makes this method viable only for large retailers capable of ordering high volume, mainly in the mass market. The latter method is employed mainly by independent stores though it can also be applicable to a lesser extent to fashion multiples – particularly department stores – and mail order companies to supplement their own ranges. Mass market retailers generally have a higher mark-up on their products than stores which sell branded merchandise despite the fact that consumers pay higher prices for branded goods.

References

Key Note (2006) *UK Clothing Manufacturing Report May 2006.* Key Note, London.
Retail Intelligence (1999) *Womenswear Retailing March 1999.* Mintel, London.
Retail Intelligence (2006) *Clothing Retailing UK September 2006.* Mintel, London.

Chapter 2

The Role of the Fashion Buyer

The buying role differs between companies but all fashion buyers are responsible for overseeing the development of a range of products aimed at a specific type of customer and price bracket. There are various levels of seniority within a buying team, ranging from small independent stores, which may have one buyer who also participates in sales and promotion, to a major fashion multiple which has trainee buyers, assistant buyers, buyers and buying managers, headed by a buying director. The job title can also vary, most notably at Marks and Spencer, where buyers are referred to as 'selectors'. Members of a buying team need to be effective communicators as most of their time at work is spent liaising with suppliers or internal departments.

Buyers usually buy merchandise for a specific product area. In a small company, this may be a very broad range, for example ladies' casualwear, including jackets, tops, skirts and trousers, but in a large multiple, the range is likely to be far more focused, for example men's shirts. Usually, the larger the company the narrower the buyer's product area is. It is probable however that a buyer for a very narrow product range in a large company will be responsible for a higher amount of financial turnover, owing to large quantities per style being sold, than a buyer for a broader product range working for a smaller retailer. If the range of product categories is large most retailers, including Marks and Spencer and Bhs, have separate buying departments or divisions for menswear, womenswear and childrenswear. The responsibility for buying merchandise is subdivided into specific product ranges which may include jerseywear, knitwear, leisurewear, nightwear, swimwear, tailoring, underwear, eveningwear, footwear and accessories. In larger companies roles are usually more strictly defined than in smaller companies where the job may be more diverse in terms of products and responsibilities, calling for versatile buyers with a wide range of skills, as the job can sometimes extend into the creative and technical areas of design and quality control.

The buying role for small independent retailers and some department stores is quite different from working for a high street fashion chain store, as independents mostly buy ranges of branded merchandise without the opportunity to become involved in the design or development of the product. The buyer's role is usually different in America as it includes more administrative duties and financial input which in the UK are normally part of the merchandiser's job (Clodfelter, 2003). In the USA buying is often a subdivision of the merchandising team, whereas in many companies in the UK buying is perceived as the central role. The experienced buyer's role invariably involves travelling, mainly to see clothing suppliers and to gather trend information (see Chapters 5, 6 and 7). A trainee buyer rarely travels abroad during the first year of employment. This gives a new recruit the chance to see how the head office operates and to assist the buyers before they embark on overseas trips. The first working trip for a trainee or assistant buyer is likely to be to Paris to view the trends at trade fairs and in stores, but after two or three years he or she can be travelling to several countries per season, depending on the retailer and the product area.

Qualities of a successful buyer

A fashion buyer needs to be versatile and flexible as the buying schedule may include sitting behind a desk one day writing reports and communicating by phone or email, travelling to Paris to identify forthcoming trends the next week, then flying to the Far East the following month to meet and negotiate with suppliers. A good buyer needs stamina but should also be enthusiastic, conscientious, professional, decisive, numerate, creative, imaginative and well motivated. To succeed in this career buyers need to have foresight and develop skills in people management and time management. It is rare to find someone with an equal balance between these qualities and skills and many buyers will excel in some while being only adequate in others. Although this list appears to be daunting, most of the skills are learnt within the job. Enthusiasm and self-motivation are possibly the most important elements as they cannot be taught; they are the main qualities that, together with experience or qualifications will help the buyer to obtain that all-important first job. It is very difficult to ascertain solely from CVs and interviews whether or not a person has the right qualities to be a buyer as most of these will only be developed by exposure to the fashion buying environment. If, however, you already have most of these qualities and the willingness to acquire the rest, you have the potential to be a successful buyer. Even with extensive skills and experience a buyer who is new to a company will require a certain period of training and readjustment to become familiar with different systems and terminology. Companies that do not recognise and plan for this factor could lower their profits as a result when the new buyer's range is launched.

Liaising with suppliers

Buyers liaise with garment suppliers on a regular, often daily, basis. A buyer may spend more time speaking to a representative from one of the company's manufacturers, probably from the design or sales department, than to another buyer from the same office. It is important therefore to establish strong working relationships with suppliers as a mutually supportive approach will be beneficial to both parties. The buyers interviewed for this book each stressed their reliance on suppliers to enable ranges to be bought successfully. Occasionally buyers appear to view themselves as being on the 'opposite side' to suppliers – in a superior position – as they have the ultimate decision-making power. However this can be detrimental to buying a successful range as the supplier may be reluctant to offer new ideas if the buyer is too autocratic. It should be remembered that retailers and manufacturers both have the same main aim: to sell as many garments as possible by meeting customers' requirements. To liaise effectively both the buyer and supplier need to form a relationship based on integrity, reliability and respect. Buyers can only expect to see samples and costings delivered on time by the manufacturer if they in turn respond quickly and professionally to the supplier's phone calls or emails. Buyers liaise with suppliers for numerous reasons throughout the buying cycle (see Chapter 3) in relation to selecting, ordering and delivery of garments and, in the case of own label retailers, participating in the product development process.

Negotiation

One of the major aspects of the buyer's role in dealing with suppliers is to negotiate prices and delivery dates, and many major retailers therefore offer training courses in negotiation skills to their buyers. The garment manufacturer's sales executive, or occasionally the senior designer, submits a 'cost price' for a garment, which has been based on the result of a costing process in the factory (see Chapter 7). This may take place in a face-to-face discussion, or in writing. The buyer calculates how much the garment needs to be sold for in the store to achieve the retailer's 'mark-up', which is the difference between the manufacturer's cost price and the selling price. The cost price is usually multiplied by around 2.5 to calculate the retail selling price for a retailer of branded goods, or three times the cost price for an own label retailer, including Value Added Tax (VAT) in the UK (see Chapter 5). It may appear from these mark-ups that retailers make a great deal of profit, but their slice of the selling price has to be substantial in order to cover overheads such as store rents, utility bills, shop assistants' wages and head office costs, including the buyer's salary, and – it is hoped – some net profit for the company.

Buyers should be able to estimate from past experience how much the consumer will expect to pay for a particular garment, and therefore can calculate the optimum cost price which they would be prepared to pay. Initially the supplier approaches the price from a different angle from that of the buyer, working on how much the garment will cost the supplier to produce. An experienced salesperson working for a manufacturer is also able to anticipate how much the buyer expects to pay. The buyer obviously wants to pay as little as possible for the product whereas the salesperson wants to sell it for as much as possible, since both are aiming to make profits for their respective companies. The buyer and salesperson both need to be realistic, however, and use their judgement as to which prices are reasonable. If the buyer cannot achieve the retailer's target margin the buying manager will probably need to give permission for the garment to be purchased at this price, otherwise the style may be dropped from the range.

Liaising with internal departments

Buying and merchandising are invariably centralised operations for retail chains, as economies of scale and higher efficiency are achieved this way. London is by far the most popular location for the head offices of British fashion retailers, though several large store chains and most mail order companies are based in the North, the Midlands or in Scotland. Fashion buyers liaise regularly with colleagues from other departments at head office, as the successful development and retailing of a fashion range is a team effort, requiring a variety of specialist input. Although buyers are usually based alongside, and interact frequently with, other members of the buying team it is likely that they will spend more working time in contact with other internal departments, as shown in Figure 2.1. This varies from one company to another as not all retailers have in-house design teams, fabric technologists or packaging teams. Buying is seen as a crucial and central role at head office, as the buyer makes key decisions about the products sold by the company and the job therefore involves liaison with most of the retailer's internal departments. The buyer may liaise frequently, on a daily or weekly basis, with key departments such as merchandising and quality control (QC), or intermittently with other departments, such as marketing.

The buying team

Buyers need to work closely with the rest of their buying colleagues, as their ranges need to be sold alongside each other in the same stores, and are likely to be purchased to be worn together. Buyers from different areas therefore need to liaise regularly to keep in touch with developments in ranges and to support each other. Most buying teams have regular, perhaps weekly, meetings

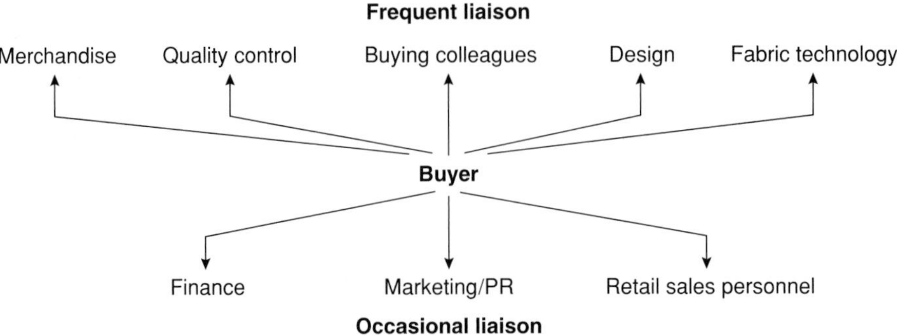

Figure 2.1 Buyer liaison with internal departments.

under the guidance of a buying manager. Some buyers may meet more often on an informal basis to update each other on ranges, and to ask for advice or opinions. If there is a quality problem with a garment in the range and the buyer does not wish to reject it, another experienced buyer's opinion may be sought to help the decision-making process. Buyers usually travel together on business trips and can therefore consult each other for advice on the range. Buyers for product ranges which are closely linked (e.g. if one is responsible for blouses and another for tailoring) are likely to consult each other frequently, to ensure that the range is well coordinated. Sometimes the buyer may need to contact another buyer in a separate division of the company, so a ladies' casualwear buyer who wants to source a certain type of fabric may seek the advice of a casualwear buyer from a menswear retailer within the same store group.

Merchandise department

The fashion buyer needs the commercial flair to buy a range, whilst the merchandiser needs the commercial acumen to enable the range to work successfully. Merchandisers interact very regularly with buyers, and are responsible for setting the financial parameters of a garment range. This can include creating a framework for the buying budget, defining the number of product types and determining the number of lines within a range. In effect merchandisers give buyers a shopping list of products in terms of prices (entry, mid or high) and the length of time which they are expected to be in store. Nick Atkinson, menswear accessories merchandiser at River Island, describes how his role works in practice:

> I sit side-by-side with the buyer and the rest of the team: working closely with an assistant merchandiser, allocator and senior allocator. My main responsibilities are minimising risk, maximising potential and planning a balanced range. We have a target of how much profit to make for the season and how much markdown we're allowed. Merchandisers need good computer skills and as the job is very numerical and analytical, being able to read figures and pull out the information is essential. Communication is also very important between the design, buying and merchandising teams.

Merchandisers have a major role to play in many of the key meetings and processes within the buying cycle (see Chapter 3). They advise buyers on target margins for the range – which may differ for certain garments depending on the country of origin, the flexibility and lead time of the supplier, and the balance of the margin across the whole range. If a product makes a lower margin than the target which has been set, it may still be approved if other products in the range make a higher margin to compensate for it. This is referred to as 'marrying' margins, and is usually acceptable if the average margin across the whole range equals or exceeds the target. Merchandisers liaise frequently with buyers and suppliers to place initial and repeat orders. This involves regular meetings with buyers to assess the progress of each style in a range, referred to as progress-chasing, with buyers overseeing most of the product development phase and merchandisers taking over at the production stage. Buyers and merchandisers may have meetings jointly with suppliers either in the UK or overseas.

Some retailers have a team of stock controllers, rather than merchandisers, who perform a similar though probably more limited role. In some companies merchandisers, rather than buyers, negotiate the volume of production allocated to the retailer for the season. The role of the merchandiser can also include contact with members of staff in stores, as well as warehousing and distribution. Some retailers also have a team – often known as allocators, optimisers or branch merchandisers – responsible for coordinating the delivery of merchandise from the warehouse to stores. A large part of the merchandiser's role is to monitor sales progress, usually from a weekly sales report. Most fashion stores have electronic point-of-sale (EPOS) systems which instantly deliver sales information from all branches to a central database each time a purchase is made by a customer, enabling merchandisers to access sales figures daily if necessary. Merchandisers take action on the basis of sales figures to order repeat deliveries from manufacturers for bestselling lines while marking down poor sellers. Ultimately merchandisers are responsible for ensuring that the product range selected and developed by the buyer is delivered to stores in the right size ratios and quantities at the right time.

Design department

Most retailers do not have in-house designers, leaving design and development to buyers, in conjunction with clothing manufacturers' design teams. However some of the major store groups in the UK employ their own designers who work closely with buyers on the design direction of the range. The retailer's design team is responsible for identifying trends which are suitable for the store for a particular season and usually design the mood boards, colour palettes and garment silhouettes (see Chapter 4) to be used by the buying team and by the clothing manufacturers which supply the retailer. This ensures a consistent direction across the whole product range and retailers such as Oasis, Next and Warehouse who operate in this way are often easily identifiable, owing to their very cohesive and directional ranges. Buyers brief designers working on the appropriate product area by requesting a new version of last season's successful black trousers, for example, or an innovative new style of top to update the range. The design team usually works within the head office building, overseen by a design manager. Locating the designers together enables them to utilise more effectively resources and equipment, such as computers, magazines and art materials.

Quality control/garment technology department

Various titles can be given for the person responsible for the technical and quality aspects of a garment range. Quality controller (QC) is one of the most popular terms, as the role involves ensuring that the garments in the buyer's range conform to the quality standards set by the retailer. Most fashion retailers have their own QCs who are based at the head office, and, like buyers, are responsible for specific product areas, such as women's leisurewear or underwear. Sometimes a buyer and QC work together on exactly the same product range, but often the QC is responsible for a larger area of merchandise, and therefore works with more than one buyer. The buyer and QC are likely to be involved together mostly in fitting sessions, which often take place on a weekly basis during key times within the season. Buyers are responsible for finalising the aesthetic aspects of the fit and shape of the garment, such as skirt length and proportion, while QCs are responsible for commenting on the technical aspects including methods of garment manufacture and the balance of the garments. The QC usually documents both the aesthetic and technical feedback from fitting sessions and communicates this information to the manufacturer. After the fit of a product has been finalised in conjunction with the buyer, the QC tends to take over the management of the product through to the production, delivery and packaging, usually only involving the buyer if any issues need to be resolved. The QC is also responsible for ensuring that garments comply with British Standards, safety regulations and legislation. QCs require a sound technical knowledge, which they may have gained from experience working for a manufacturer and/or a technically-biased fashion degree, as well as by using effective communication and organisational skills.

Fabric technology department

Only the larger-scale retailers, such as Marks and Spencer, employ their own fabric technologists. In most other stores the QC department is responsible for checking the quality of fabrics. Fabric technologists are usually involved in sourcing and developing fabrics with suppliers in conjunction with the buying team and are responsible for ensuring that fabrics that go into production meet the retailer's quality standards. Most fabric technologists have a specialist degree in textile technology. Some retailers have their own laboratories where fabric technologists are responsible for testing fabrics from samples and bulk production but this is extremely rare as laboratories are expensive owing to the equipment and space required. Most of the testing for fabrics for the high street is carried out by specialist companies which have been formally approved by the retailer's fabric technology or QC department. Garment manufacturers are usually expected to pay for fabric testing.

Occasionally garment suppliers have their own in-house laboratories which are approved to test fabric to the retailer's standards. This can be more economical for larger companies than the expense of sending every fabric to an independent testing house. Fabric technologists who work for retailers are responsible for checking that the fabric for every garment which goes into production meets the retailer's standards and they may also be responsible for setting those standards. If a fabric is slightly below the required standard after it has been produced and is ready to be made into garments the fabric technologist will probably consult the buyer, as rejecting it could mean that delivery would be delayed for several weeks leaving a gap in the buyer's range. This is a challenging decision for the buyer, who may choose to take the risk that there will be slightly higher garment returns due to imperfections in the fabric, rather than miss out on potential sales. One way of minimising the risk is to have some garments made up in the fabric and to ask a few people to wear them for a certain amount of time (a 'wearer trial') to see how severe the problem is likely to be.

Other departments

The majority of the buyer's internal meetings are with merchandise, QC and design. Other departments tend to be in less regular contact with the buying team, some as little as once a season. Most buyers have some involvement with promoting the range in conjunction with the marketing or public relations (PR) department. Garments which appear in magazines are often initial samples made before the products are manufactured in bulk, and these need to be ordered from the supplier by the buyer. The buyer may work with the finance department when planning budgets to ensure sufficient money is available and to check exchange rates when buying merchandise from overseas. Some larger retailers have specialist departments to organise the importation of merchandise and they may need to inform the buyer if a problem arises, such as a delivery being delayed in customs. The retailer may have its own legal department or use independent legal advice which the buyer may need to consult, for instance if a competing store appears to have copied the retailer's merchandise. The buyer also needs to liaise with support staff at head office including the reception desk, administrators and catering staff, who should be treated with equal respect as they can all be of help in enabling the buyer's schedule to run smoothly. The buyer may also be required to meet staff from the company's stores to introduce the new range to sales staff. Some retailers have their own offices overseas so they can liaise with garment suppliers in those countries and buyers whose ranges are produced abroad are likely to be in frequent contact with members of staff in these offices.

Management skills

Most buyers have management responsibilities for junior staff such as trainee or assistant buyers and buying administrators. Some companies give training to buyers to prepare them for a management role, but many do not. Buyers are often promoted because of their ability to buy successful, profitable ranges, though this may not mean that they automatically have the skills to manage others. If the company does not offer training, a buyer who has been promoted may wish to gain management knowledge by studying if time allows. There are numerous books about management which can equip buyers with relevant skills relatively quickly and easily. The buyer could also initiate informal management training by arranging to meet more experienced colleagues who can share their experiences and approaches to managing a team. Interviewing potential assistant buyers is often part of the buyer's role, which requires effective planning and preparation skills.

Buyers may draw from their own experiences of being managed at a junior level and view management from the perspective of their assistants, treating their staff professionally and supportively, as they would expect to be treated. One of the most frequent problems for assistant buyers is being inadequately briefed about buying tasks, since buyers may presume assistants to be more knowledgeable than they actually are and briefing time is limited. The buyer must maintain an approachable attitude, and ensure that sufficient time is devoted to briefing. Although it is difficult to find time in a busy buying department the consequences of not doing so can be that mistakes will be made, and the buyer should be prepared to take responsibility for errors if assistants are not adequately informed. A well-motivated, well-briefed assistant can save the buyer a lot of time by making the job run more smoothly, but an assistant who is demoralised by a lack of information can quickly become demotivated and less productive and may eventually resign, causing the buyer to go through the time-consuming and expensive recruitment process again. If an assistant buyer encounters such problems, it is worth telling the buyer assertively but politely that more information is needed, with a brief example of a problem that could have been avoided. The buyer may not even have realised that a problem existed, and a professional buyer will be grateful for the discussion and act upon it. If the buyer does not respond well to this information and poor briefings continue to cause mistakes which are blamed upon the assistant, it may be time for the assistant either to discuss the situation with the personnel department or the buyer's line manager, or to request a transfer to another product area. Buyers should treat all colleagues professionally at whatever level; they should note that most assistants will be in senior positions some day and may be encountered by the buyer in another company at a later stage. One of the most difficult aspects of the transition from buyer to buying manager can be to delegate the hands-on aspects of buying and allow the buyers to be responsible for most of their own decisions on products.

As well as being responsible for managing staff a buyer also manages a range of garments, a budget, resources including space within the buying department, and time. To manage these elements effectively the buyer needs to communicate well with a variety of people. It is important for the buyer to meet with staff on a regular basis and a weekly meeting at a set time with assistant and trainee buyers is usually an effective way to manage. The meetings should take place at a regular time, ideally for one to two hours, in an office where the team will not be interrupted. (Remember that if you stop to take a phone call for half an hour and there are four of you in the meeting, you will have wasted two hours of the team's potential time in total.) Set an agenda for the meeting and keep to it, while still giving the rest of the team the opportunity to bring up relevant issues. If an issue needs to be discussed at length with only one assistant arrange to talk about this later rather than using up the whole team's time in the meeting. Key points for discussion should include a review of events and tasks during the previous week and the anticipated tasks for the coming week. Action points should be noted, with a member of the team being nominated for responsibility for each task. The team should be made to feel able to raise any problems that are hindering their work and the buyer should be responsible for taking steps to alleviate these problems rather than simply considering the team to have a negative approach. In this way complaints can be turned around into positive outcomes if the buyer is willing to listen and act accordingly. It is also essential to put positive items on the agenda, such as good sales figures and successes within the team. Too often we are dismissive of success, and concentrate on problems instead; achievements should be celebrated in order to maintain and boost morale. Try to leave as much time as reasonably possible at the end of the meeting before making other appointments as the meetings may occasionally need to run over time to address issues.

A single meeting is unlikely to be sufficient to deal with all of the issues which arise during the week. The buyer needs to communicate with the team on at least a daily basis. The buyer should ensure that assistants are not afraid to initiate discussions when required. The buyer also needs time in private to plan and organise, and may wish to set aside a period to be undisturbed by the team unless an emergency arises. If the buyer has identified a problem with an assistant's performance this should always be dealt with privately and at a reasonably early stage so that the problem does not worsen. This can be difficult to achieve as many buying offices are open plan but a compromise could be made by having the discussion when there are fewer people than usual in the office, or by booking a meeting room. The buyer should give the assistant clear, attainable objectives to improve performance within a set time. After the stated time the buyer should review the assistant's performance and either offer praise if the situation has improved sufficiently or reset objectives. Sometimes the buyer may be able to solve the problem once the cause has been established, if it is within the workplace, or offer moral support if it is the result of a personal issue. Buyers occasionally receive complaints about how the team operates from members of other head office departments. The buyer should discuss these issues with the team and if necessary invite the complainant to a meeting to discuss the problem openly, with the aim of resolving the situation.

The management methods detailed above may be possible in an ideal situation but the buying environment has many constraints, particularly lack of time. It will not always be possible to be consistently good at both buying and management, but if you take a genuine interest in your staff and appreciate how important their support is to your own success at work, you have the capacity to become an effective manager. Management skills, like buying skills, need to be learned, and should eventually become as natural as buying a garment range.

Summary

The role of the buyer is to develop a range of products appropriate for the retailer's market, by:

- liaising regularly with suppliers, in the UK or overseas
- liaising regularly with internal departments, including other buyers, merchandisers and QCs
- managing junior staff.

The qualities required of the buyer to fulfil this role include:

- stamina
- enthusiasm and motivation
- product knowledge
- creativity.

Reference

Clodfelter, R. (2003) *Retail Buying: from Basics to Fashion*. Fairchild, New York.

Chapter 3

The Buying Cycle

The fashion industry traditionally splits the year into two main seasons: spring/summer (February to July) and autumn/winter (August to January). The competitive and constantly changing fashion business requires a more frequent injection of merchandise, resulting in most stores introducing new products at least once a month. The buying cycle refers to the key events and processes in which the fashion buyer is involved in order to buy a garment range in for a retail or mail order company. Figure 3.1 lists the main events in the buying

Task	Approximate date
Review of current season's sales	early August
↓	
Budget planning	mid-August
↓	
Comparative shopping	August–September
↓	
Directional shopping	August–October
↓	
(Fabric sourcing)	October–December
↓	
Range planning	October–November
↓	
Garment sourcing	November
↓	
(Pre-selection)	early December
↓	
Price negotiation with suppliers	November–December
↓	
Final range selection	mid-December
↓	
Placing orders for ranges	December–January
↓	
(Product development – sample fittings, fabric testing)	January–April
↓	
Bulk garment manufacture	April–July
↓	
Delivery of products to retailer	August
↓	
PURCHASE BY CUSTOMER	August–October

Figure 3.1 An example of the buying cycle for a Phase 1 autumn/winter range.

cycle chronologically. The length of the buying cycle varies between companies but usually takes a year between reviewing the current season's sales and delivering into stores. For example, in August a buyer may review the current year's spring/summer sales and begin directional shopping to inspire concepts for the autumn/winter range for the following year.

Although the buying cycle for a whole season's range can take up to a year, it is usual to develop smaller ranges and individual garments more quickly. Buyers are increasingly keeping a substantial percentage of the season's budget available (referred to as the 'open-to-buy') to respond to trends by purchasing 'fast fashion' items. Zara, Topshop, H&M and George have become renowned for spearheading this phenomenon, devoting a high percentage of their budgets to products with short turnaround times and high fashionability, motivating other retailers to follow suit. Mail order companies have to contend with ordering products earlier than most bricks-and-mortar retailers, to accommodate the time for a photo shoot to take place (see Chapter 8). Some have responded to the demand for fast fashion by holding back some of the open-to-buy for certain garments (called 'held options') to be photographed on a second, smaller shoot, at the latest possible date for inclusion in the catalogue or website.

For retailers aiming at the more fashion-conscious younger end of the market the whole buying cycle is usually much shorter than a year, in order to respond to trends rapidly. This can sometimes reduce the quality of the merchandise as speed of manufacture may take priority, but being able to buy a current fashion item at a competitive price is probably more important to the target customer. The time taken to make bulk orders of garments can vary greatly but as a rough estimate, production of fabric can take about six weeks, and manufacture of a single style may take about four weeks. This is a very simplistic calculation, as there are many other factors which affect the time from order to delivery of products. As most garments sold in the UK are imported, transport time needs to be built in. The manufacture of each style needs to be planned into a factory's production schedule, and this can result in a gap between arrival of the fabric and the commencement of bulk production.

It is essential to remember that the intended outcome of the buying cycle is that the customer will want to purchase the products, so the requirements of the potential customer must be taken into consideration by the buyer at every stage. The features in brackets in Figure 3.1 are the responsibility only of buyers who become involved in product development and would not be relevant to retailers who buy branded ranges for either department stores or smaller, independent stores. The dates included are for guidance only and will vary between companies. Some of the more basic or classic products within a range may be sold from August to January, with fashion items being available for between one and three months.

Though the buying cycle can take up to a year there are obviously two main ranges to be bought annually, so the buyer is always working on at least two seasons' ranges simultaneously. While the buyer is planning a range for the autumn/winter season, garment fittings and approvals of fabric colour and quality are still under way for the spring/summer season. Most fashion buyers now buy ranges more frequently than twice per year as an autumn/winter range has to change in order to meet customers' needs effectively from August to January in terms of both climate and fashionability. It is usual for most UK fashion retailers to introduce new ranges (sometimes referred to as phases) to stores at least once a month and some trend-led stores are known for their weekly injections of fresh stock. This does not mean completely changing the range, but frequently introducing new fashion items whilst retaining bestsellers and/or basic lines in store. Ranges which bridge the gap between one season and the next are called 'transitional', accounting for the fact that the spring season is actually launched during winter (in February) and the autumn range during summer (August). This makes the fashion buying environment extremely challenging as the workload for two or three seasons overlaps, leaving no time to pause in between new ranges.

Review of current season's sales and budget planning

The buyer constantly reviews sales figures, which are available at least once a week, to be aware of how a garment range is performing. The merchandise department usually takes responsibility for compiling a review of the whole previous season's performance of the range so that the bestsellers and poor sellers (dogs) can be identified. This review often takes the form of a presentation to the buying team (and the design department if the company has one) with samples of garments from the range being shown and analysed. This may be known as a sales review or range direction meeting. Assistant buyers may be asked to help organise this presentation by acquiring relevant garment samples. The QC department may contribute to the meeting by commenting on any technical problems which may explain low sales figures, for instance the colour or fit in production differing from the catalogue photograph of the garment. Alternatively the QC department may organise a separate presentation to discuss garment quality issues.

After the review of sales figures buyers are armed with knowledge of which styles the customer currently likes and dislikes and a framework of successes to build upon for the new season, so a rough idea of the new range plan can start to be pencilled in. They may also be able to learn from other buyers' sales figures, so if a new fabric or colour has been trialled in another product area the buyer can decide whether or not to run it too. The buyer may instinctively avoid including in the new range a version of a garment which has previously sold poorly, but this needs to be viewed within the context of current trends. It is possible that the style was offered too early for the customer, so this type of garment should not be completely dismissed. Low sales could also be caused by low quality standards of fabric or garment manufacture and the buyer may therefore choose to buy a similar style from a different supplier as a result. If a garment has sold particularly well the buyer will probably decide to run one or more versions of this style in the next season. However the buyer could alternatively view the bestseller as a short-term fad and decide not to run it again.

Merchandisers usually plan budgets in conjunction with buyers. The framework for the budget is based largely on the last season's performance as discussed at the range review, as well as any anticipated developments. For example, if tailoring is predicted to be a major trend for a future season and dressing casually is considered to have reached the peak of its sales potential, the tailoring budget may be increased and the investment in the leisurewear range reduced accordingly. The buyer should be far more informed about this type of fashion trend than the merchandising or finance departments and therefore needs to utilise this information to influence budget-setting.

Even before design concepts have been developed it is possible to estimate the total value of a range by defining the number of styles with provisional quantities. The merchandise department may construct the price architecture of the range by planning the number of styles per retail selling price. The finance department may also be involved in budget planning as they should be aware of the amount of money that the company has available to purchase future ranges. Assistant buyers are rarely involved in budget planning, as this is one of the managerial roles of buyers and buying managers.

Comparative shopping

Comparative shopping is often referred to as 'comp. shop', and is usually undertaken at the beginning of each season by the buying and/or design teams. This means looking at current merchandise in the stores of competitors which sell comparable ranges (similar product types and prices). A report is often produced after the comp. shop visit, to be distributed amongst the team. This may include some sketches and often takes the form of a grid with descriptions of products compared with prices, fabrics and colours of similar merchandise from competing stores. A conclusion may be added analysing how the competitors' ranges compare with each other and noting any important trends or styles which are missing from the buyer's range so that this may be acted upon quickly. Some stores compile comp. shop reports at least once a month and this can often be one of the first tasks given to trainee buyers to familiarise them with competitors in the same market.

Directional shopping

'Directional shopping' is the term used for trips to gain inspiration for design concepts for a new season. Many buyers visit cities such as Paris, London, Milan and New York for directional shopping trips, depending on the company's travel budget. The choice of locations to visit also depends on the buyer's product range. Florence and Brussels are popular for childrenswear whereas Paris is appropriate for all types of men's, women's and children's merchandise.

During a trip, the buyer visits stores which are more directional than his or her own range, stocking merchandise following trends ahead of the buyer's own company. Most of the stores visited usually stock designer ready-to-wear ranges but buyers may also visit mass market stores which are aimed at a younger market or are more expensive than the buyer's own range, as they are also likely to stock influential styles. The buyer makes notes on key shapes, details, colour and fabric for reference, and after visiting several stores a picture will start to emerge of the key trends which are coming through. Buyers are usually given a budget to buy garments during directional shopping trips, and these are referred to as bought samples, which typify the key trends.

Retailers invest a substantial amount of money in directional shopping trips and so the schedule has to be strategically planned beforehand, to maximise the use of time. This involves deciding which areas of the city to visit and allowing time to travel between one area and another. It is often more economical to visit several countries consecutively; a trip to Europe for a childrenswear buyer could include a weekend in Paris followed by a day in Brussels and two days in Florence.

Though they may sound potentially glamorous, business trips always take up some of the buyer's own free time and many visits include weekends for which time off in lieu is unlikely to be given. During a trip the buyer will usually visit the shops as soon as they open and continue working until closing time, absorbing as much information as possible. Directional shopping is viewed as one of the most exciting aspects of the buyer's role but it can also be one of the most tiring parts of the job. During the evening the buyer is unlikely to be able to rest as this is a time to meet up with colleagues to review the day's work and sometimes provides an opportunity to socialise.

Such trips can often be viewed by other colleagues as holidays for the buying team, but it is unfair to make this comparison. Some trips abroad can be as short as one day with the buyer taking an early morning flight and returning to work in the office the next day. In certain companies designers may take the responsibility for directional shopping and often buyers and designers travel together. Buyers' directional shopping trips are becoming more restricted owing to the worldwide availability of information on designer ranges on the internet and tighter travel budgets. The subscription fee to a website such as wgsn.com which offers the subscriber access to photographs of designer collections and store windows from around the world can prove to be cheaper and less time-consuming than sending a team of buyers abroad (see Chapter 3).

Range planning and selection

Range planning is the stage when buyers define the detail of the range that is to be offered to the customer in terms of styling, fabric, design details, suppliers and prices (described in detail in Chapter 5). Many buyers do not become directly involved in fabric sourcing as garment suppliers are usually responsible for this, but buyers can make decisions regarding the selection of fabric for garments (see Chapter 6). Some buyers visit *Première Vision*, the major international fabric trade fair held in Paris twice annually, to gain an overview of fabric and colour trends (see Chapter 3). This is often combined with a directional shopping trip to Paris.

By definition all fashion buyers are required to source garments. Sometimes the garments are designed by the retailer's in-house design team but more frequently they are created by designers working for garment suppliers. Buyers may purchase garments from the supplier's original designs or may develop garments in conjunction with the manufacturer (see Chapter 7). When the buyers have completed the range planning stage, a pre-selection meeting takes place where buyers present garment samples for the range to their buying, merchandise and QC teams. Departmental managers may attend this pre-selection meeting to offer a critique on aspects such as styling, colour and price. The overall strategy for the season and supplier base may be discussed within the meeting. Numerous amendments are likely to be made to a range at pre-selection as it is the first opportunity for the buying team to gain an overview of the whole department's products. Buyers must anticipate changes to garments at pre-selection and learn not to take them personally, as the intention of any amendments should be to improve potential sales to customers. Buyers should be prepared to justify all decisions in relation to the garments where necessary and to fight (diplomatically) for the inclusion of those styles which they consider to have the potential to be bestsellers.

The period immediately after pre-selection can be the busiest time of the year as buyers often have only two weeks or less to prepare for the most important meeting of the season: final range selection. Most of the work involves contacting suppliers to explain that some garments will not be included within the range, others added, and existing styles amended. Prices may need to be renegotiated if garments have been shortened, fabrics changed or trims removed. New samples may be requested, and the range plan rewritten to include the changes. The final range selection meeting gives buyers the opportunity to present the range in its entirety with product samples for each style. Chasing initial samples from suppliers can make this a stressful though exciting time, and if garments miss the deadline they are unlikely to be included within the final range. It is rarely possible for all of the samples at the final range selection to be in the correct colour as the fabric needs to be dyed to the retailer's requested colour in bulk production, which cannot be done until the final order has been placed. Garments are usually shown in the correct fabric quality with swatches of colourways attached, and certain styles may be shown on live models. Final range selection usually takes less time than pre-selection as much of the groundwork has already been done, and it provides an opportunity to sign off some garments and make slight amendments to others. As most high street retailers introduce new ranges at least once a month, selection meetings can take place twelve times or more per year.

After range selection meetings initial orders are sent to suppliers and then contracts for all products within the range are completed. 'New line sheets' (sometimes called purchase sheets) are generated by buyers and merchandisers for each item which has been selected for inclusion in the final range. Such documentation is usually completed using a computer, with templates or software which are often unique to the retailer. Details on the new line sheet can include the buyer's signature, the retailer's style reference number, the season, the manufacturer and country of origin, the manufacturer's style reference number, the cost price, retail selling price, yarn or fabric fibre content and construction (weight and/or gauge), size range, colour/s, description, sketch, delivery/shipping date. Initial order quantities are usually specified through discussions between the buyer and merchandiser, sometimes using a process referred to as 'ranking'. This involves reviewing samples of each style in the range and estimating their potential sales figures, consequently ordering larger quantities of those styles which are ranked most highly. The new line sheet is signed off by the buying manager if all of the details are approved, and then distributed to other departments within the company including QC, and the supplier, or can be accessed from the company's intranet, as a definitive record of the style. If amendments need to be made to the style, for instance cancelling one of the colourways, this needs to be documented and may require signing off by the buying manager.

Critical paths for product development, production and delivery

The schedule of key dates for product development and production is known as the 'critical path' because it is critical that these deadlines are met if the range is to be launched into stores by the intended date. The key dates for the season are usually planned by senior managers such as the buying director and merchandise manager. These dates are communicated to the buying and merchandise teams in order to plan visits and meetings with relevant departments and suppliers. The schedule is usually planned in reverse chronological order, beginning with the launch date of the range and working back to the deadlines necessary to achieve delivery on time. Consistent lateness on the part of the buyer, designer or manufacturer in developing and approving various aspects of each garment by critical dates would result in garments not being available to customers at the required time and lead to reduced profits for the company. The buyer needs to compile a critical path (see Table 3.1) for every garment in the range to be able to successfully monitor progress, which may be carried out using a specialist computer program. This includes deadline dates for such factors as testing of the fabric quality at sample and bulk stage, approval of the colour for fabric, fastenings and trims, and fitting the garment. The buyer should aim to have each of these elements approved prior to the required deadline to allow for any rejections and resubmissions of fabrics, trims or fitting samples. The majority of fitting samples will not be approved first time as the buyer may choose to amend the proportion and styling and the QC will probably alter the fit.

The buyer should be sufficiently familiar with the quality standards of the suppliers to anticipate how long it might take to complete all of the relevant

Table 3.1 Example of a critical path chart for the approval of garment styles.
SEASON: autumn/winter. Critical path last updated: 26 March

Style No	Description	Supplier and country of origin	Lab-dye/ strike-off approval	Sample fabric approval	Trim approval	Size 12 fitting sample approval	Grades approval sizes 8,12,16	Bulk fabric and trim approval	Bulk production starts	Due in warehouse
AW028	Long sleeve red top	TL Co Hong Kong	✓Approved 24/1	✓Approved 22/1	✓Approved 25/1	Rejected 23/3 – second sample due 1/4	Due 14/4	Due 23/4	1/5	10/8
AW029	Blue vest	BY Ltd UK	✓Approved 14/2	Rejected 6/2 – new sample due 25/2	✓Approved 15/3	✓Approved 25/3	Due 30/4	Due 14/5	28/6	10/8

approvals and build in time for the possibility of samples being rejected and resubmitted. However this can be difficult to predict as most styles have never been made in production before with exactly the same fabric, colour and styling details. This makes fashion merchandise notoriously unpredictable in terms of quality as production runs are short-term, usually lasting only a few weeks or days. This is in contrast to products in many other industries where merchandise tends to be produced over a much longer period of time, allowing many initial production problems to be eliminated.

Monitoring the critical path of a garment range is one of the major responsibilities of the buyer and also forms a large part of the role of an assistant (or trainee) buyer. Most fashion buyers are responsible for over a hundred garment styles within a range, including merchandise for more than one season at a time so it is essential that progress is documented as it would be impossible to rely solely on an individual's memory. Manufacturers need to be notified of all the key dates for approval for each garment within the range. Once a style has been selected the buyer or merchandiser gives it a reference number to ensure easier communication and to avoid errors. Even though suppliers should be aware of dates by which fabric, trim or garment samples should be submitted for approval, buyers or their assistants frequently have to chase progress by contacting manufacturers to check when the samples will be submitted, often because they are late. Buyers therefore need to have good verbal and written communication skills. Skills of diplomacy are also required as the buyer/supplier relationship is mutually beneficial, and a reprimand from the buyer for late delivery of a sample may be inappropriate if the supplier meets deadlines 95% of the time. Buyers need suppliers and vice versa, and it is not worth jeopardising the relationship because of an occasional mistake. The buyer or assistant buyer will probably have a weekly meeting with the merchandiser working on the same product range in order to update each other on progress on the critical path.

Some stores use computer systems to monitor critical paths, which can be updated as progress is made and accessed via a network which reduces the need for meetings. The buying manager may also request a regular review of the range's progress with the buyer and may be called upon to intervene if problems arise with particular styles or suppliers.

Approval of fabric and trims

After a buyer has selected a garment in a specific fabric to be included within a range, most retailers have stringent procedures to which the buyer, QC and supplier must adhere to ensure suitable quality standards. The garment will have been shown at a range presentation made from a sample length of fabric. The garment manufacturer has to have the sample fabric tested at an approved laboratory (see below). The buyer will probably have requested the garment to be dyed to a specific shade from the retailer's colour palette for the relevant season, so the fabric manufacturer will have dyed a swatch of the fabric to this shade. This swatch is known as a 'lab dye' (or lab dip) and is usually sent to the buyer for approval. The buyer looks at the lab dye in a light box (a small booth containing light bulbs usually of the same type as used in the retailer's stores) to demonstrate how the colour will appear to the customer when making a purchase. The lab dye is compared to the original colour swatch to which the buyer requested the fabric to be matched. Each lab dye is given a reference number which is a record of the exact recipe used to achieve the shade (the proportions of dyes which were mixed together) to ensure that the buyer can give approval without needing to return the swatch. The buyer should immediately write the date on the card to which the lab dye is attached and whether it is approved or rejected.

If a lab dye is rejected it is important that the buyer gives feedback to the manufacturer about the nature of the problem: for instance a purple shade may need to have slightly more red added to it to match correctly. It is important that all lab dyes for a particular shade are matched to the original swatch from the colour palette as there will probably be several garments in the store at the same time, possibly from different buyers' ranges, and it is important that the shade is consistent to ensure that garments match each other. One buyer could have a shirt made in fabric from Turkey in the same shade of blue as a pair of trousers made in fabric from China in another buyer's range. Because of the vast distance between the fabric producers, who are not in contact with each other, the buyers need to be the link controlling the consistency of the colour, or sales may be lost due to incorrect matching of shades.

Although it may seem insignificant if a shade of blue is very slightly darker than the original swatch it is essential to correct this as another fabric manufacturer may have produced a lab dye slightly lighter than the original, resulting in garments clashing if these shades are approved to go into mass production. Sometimes the fabric supplier may send the buyer several lab dyes for approval so that the closest one can be selected immediately without the need for resubmission if the first one is rejected. For a printed fabric the buyer may select a colourway from the supplier's range or ask for the colours to be based on the retailer's own colour palette. The manufacturer usually sends the buyer a 'strike-off' for approval, which is a large swatch of the fabric printed in the requested colours. Suppliers also send swatches of bulk fabric from production for approval, and the buyer will compare these with the original colour and the approved lab dye before garment production can commence.

Fabric testing

Most fashion retailers require fabrics to be tested to check that the quality meets the company's requirements and to supply appropriate washing instructions with the garment. Large retailers may have in-house fabric quality testing facilities, but most retailers rely either on garment manufacturers' own quality laboratories or use independent testing labs. Such laboratories have full documentation of the retailer's requirements and are audited regularly to ensure adherence to the correct standards and procedures. Tests are carried out on a sample length of fabric to give an indication of its performance prior to bulk production. A sample fabric which does not pass the stated test criteria at this stage is unlikely to go into bulk production unless the fabric manufacturer can supply an improved sample. Alternatively, if the fabric is a 'must-have' product, the buyer may reconsider the criteria and accept that the garment will have to be hand-washed rather than offer the usual machine-washing instructions that the customer expects. After fabric quality testing, washing instructions are issued by the retailer's fabric technology or QC department and these will be incorporated in the garment label. Because of retailers' differing quality specifications the same fabric could have varying washing instructions, with a recommendation for machine wash from one retailer and handwash from another.

Garment fittings

Garments are fitted on a model of the retailer's standard size (usually size 12 for womenswear, size 42 for menswear and age 7/8 for childrenswear). Wherever possible the same model is used each time as the fit may vary on different models and lead to confusion. Some retailers keep their own house models and this used to be standard practice for many fashion companies. Now, with tighter budgets, this tends to be restricted to larger stores which can justify a full-time model. Most retailers now hire freelance models from agencies who are paid at a daily rate. QCs may also use mannequins (life-size padded dummies of the torso) occasionally for fittings, which can either be bought in a standard size or manufactured to the retailer's exact specifications. However, it is obviously essential to see every garment on the body to be able to observe how it looks when worn, as well as checking practicalities such as whether or not it is practical for getting into and for walking around. As manufacturing is increasingly based overseas the comments on fittings need to be extremely clear and usually include helpful diagrams. English may not be the recipient's first language. Sometimes a representative from the garment manufacturer – a designer, garment technologist or pattern-cutter – will be present at the fitting if the manufacturer is based in the same country. This system enables the manufacturer's representative to be actively involved in the fitting and to offer solutions to any problems with the fit. This can minimise the number of fitting sessions before approval of the garment.

Manufacturers make amendments to the pattern and garment after a first-fit session – as the style is rarely approved first time – then submit a second sample for the next fitting session. Once the fit has been approved suppliers are usually requested to submit two identical samples in the correct fabric and the QC is responsible for sealing them by attaching the retailer's seal of approval, with notes on minor amendments required, signed and dated. One sealing sample is returned to the manufacturer before the patterns are produced in the full range of sizes which have been ordered (grades) and the other is retained by the retailer, to compare with production styles at a later stage. Some retailers request a selection of garments in different sizes, usually in the smallest, middle and largest sizes, for fitting sessions.

The main responsibility for further development of the garments is passed on from the buyer to the QC department after fittings have been finalised unless the garment technologist finds a problem on which the buyer's opinion is needed. The QC's responsibilities include checking the quality of garments during production and after delivery. Liaison with the buyer is then usually limited to updating progress on approval of grades and consultation if any problems arise. The QC's role is likely to include travelling overseas to observe a selection of garments in production. This is known as an 'in-work check', involving looking at merchandise which is currently being manufactured to check quality standards before the products are delivered to the retailer's warehouse. This helps to ensure that quality is maintained and can save the time and expense of returning low-quality merchandise to the manufacturer. Quality inspections include measuring various dimensions of the garment to ensure that they meet the required specifications and checking the quality of manufacture. Increasingly suppliers are being requested to self-certify production standards, to reduce the amount of time and money spent by retailers on carrying out in-work checks. Some retailers carry out wearer trials on all garments, but most companies do this only where potential problems are anticipated. The QC is responsible for organising wearer trials by distributing the garments to suitable wearers, gaining feedback, compiling the results and taking appropriate action where required.

It is usually not feasible for the QC to see every style in the range in production because too many styles are being made in a variety of locations. If there has not been an in-work check the manufacturer may be asked to send one or more samples from production directly to the retailer's QC department for approval before delivery. When the production of the garments is complete they are delivered to the retailer's warehouse. QCs often travel from head office to the warehouse (which is usually in a separate location) to check the quality of stock which has been delivered prior to its delivery to stores. Staff responsible for checking quality may also be employed in the retailer's warehouse, liaising with the central QC department. Normally garments are checked at random, and as few as one garment in every hundred will be inspected. However, some garments may need 100% inspection at the warehouse, if for example the supplier has had quality problems. If the quality is below standard the whole delivery could be rejected and returned to the supplier, or the buyer could be consulted to see whether or not the problem is considered to be sufficiently serious to end up being short of stock in the stores. A good QC can be an asset to the buyer, helping to eliminate potential production problems before they arise, by anticipating them at an early stage. It is beneficial for the buyer to consider advice from the QC department carefully and take this into account when making decisions relating to the development and fit of garments. Once products have been delivered to the retailer's warehouse and approved for quality they are distributed to the stores to which they have been allocated by the merchandise team. Buyers then wait in anticipation for the customers' response to the range, and sales figures are reviewed at the commencement of a new buying cycle.

Summary

The buying cycle varies between companies, but usually contains the following main elements:

- review of previous season's sales
- budget planning
- range planning
- garment sourcing
- range selection
- garment production
- delivery to stores.

Chapter 4

Predicting Fashion Trends

The buyer's job involves predicting trends for future seasons, appropriate to the product range and the potential customer. The ability to forecast fashion trends is necessary because the design, development and production of most garments take several months, so product concepts are usually initiated anywhere between two weeks and a year prior to going on sale. The buyer therefore needs to predict what the retailer's customers will want to buy well in advance of the selling period. Fortunately fashion forecasting is not simply guesswork as there are numerous different sources of inspiration for garment trends. The extent to which buyers are involved in fashion forecasting varies, but they will certainly be required to decide which trends are appropriate for their customers as an integral part of selecting a garment range. The buyer is responsible for observing, rather than creating, trend information from a variety of sources in order to select suitable looks. This information comprises garment types, silhouettes, details, trims, fabric types and colours.

Sources of fashion forecasting information

Buyers can collate forecasting information from many sources and the major ones are described below. Buyers also often acquire trend information through informal observations of fashions being adopted by the general public. The combination of sources of fashion forecasting information used as inspiration by the buyer will depend on the prediction strategy adopted by the retailer and the potential customer at whom the range is aimed.

Fashion forecasting packages and magazines

Specialist fashion forecasting companies are located in many of the major fashion cities including Paris, Milan, London, New York and Amsterdam. The packages are usually produced as printed and bound publications containing mainly visual information, such as garment sketches of key shapes and details, trend boards, colours and fabrics/yarns. Some of the main companies in this market include Promostyl, located in Paris, and Amsterdam-based Nelly Rodi. Fashion forecasting companies employ teams of designers who compile trends inspired mainly by designer-level and street fashion, social and cultural elements such as travel destinations, films and other mass media, as well as retro looks from previous decades. Fashion forecasting packages are published up to 18 months ahead of a season which makes them extremely valuable when trying to predict trends relatively far ahead of production. They are often split into various separate publications with specialisms such as menswear, lingerie or knitwear. The packages are usually published every six months and purchased by annual subscription, either directly from the company or through an agent, many of which currently cost several hundred pounds (sterling). Prices vary depending on how many sections of the fashion forecasting package are bought by a company. Some forecasting companies give presentations to key customers when new packages are introduced, and send updates nearer to the season.

A cheaper option for obtaining fashion forecasting information is to purchase specialist magazines such as *International Textiles* and *Textile View*. These publications focus primarily on fabrics and colour, but also include styling information. They are published monthly and can be bought from agents or news-stands in some of the major fashion-orientated cities. Forecasts from this type of magazine tend to be closer to the season and far less detailed than fashion forecasting packages, but they offer trend information within a suitable timescale for most buyers. Fashion trade magazines such as *Drapers* (UK) also contain fashion forecasting information, often in the form of reports from trade fairs. The internet has become increasingly important for the distribution of fashion forecasting. Its immediacy in offering information to the customer gives it an advantage over printed publications, which take longer to publish. In 1998 *Worth Global Style Network* launched a subscription-only website wgsn.com, offering a range of fashion predictions including menswear, womenswear, childrenswear, intimate apparel and knitwear (see Figure 4.1) which is now owned by the publisher and trade fair organiser EMAP. As well as predicting trends the wgsn website contains a variety of useful information

Figure 4.1 Forecasting page from wgsn.com. Courtesy of wgsn.

for the fashion buyer including a directory of manufacturers, maps of stores in fashion districts around the world, and extensive coverage of designer collections which goes on-line within days of the runway shows. The range of information on offer has made subscription to wgsn essential for many fashion retailers and suppliers. In certain companies wgsn has replaced overseas trips as the main source of forecasting. (A version of the website is available free to students on relevant courses.)

Fashion trade fairs

Trade fairs usually take place every six months, covering specialist areas of the fashion industry. Buyers visit those events which are most relevant to their product area and potential market. The most significant international fashion trade fair for fabrics is *Première Vision* (PV) which is held in Paris in March and October each year. Hundreds of fabric manufacturers and agents exhibit their latest ranges on individual stands at this enormous exhibition. There is also a central trend area where predicted colour palettes are displayed alongside examples of relevant fabrics from some of the exhibitors. An audio-visual presentation illustrates the moods of the predicted fashion trends. The Indigo section of the exhibition includes print companies selling their new ranges of designs. Many retailers and manufacturers use a visit to PV as the starting point for developing a new season's range, as the February/March exhibition includes fabrics for the following spring/summer and the next year's autumn/winter fabric collections are shown in September or October. PV usually takes place from Friday to Monday, resulting in many buyers spending a working weekend in Paris.

There are many specialist trade fairs for different market sectors, including the *Salon International de la Lingerie* for underwear ranges and *Interfilière* for underwear fabrics. In January these two complementary shows take place at the same time and location in Paris as the childrenswear fair *Mode Enfantine* and the footwear show *Salon International de la Chaussure*. Yarn shows such as *Pitti Filati* (which is based in Florence and is aimed at the knitwear industry) tend to take place earlier than fabric or clothing trade fairs as yarn is the first item to be manufactured in the chain of garment production.

There are many shows specialising in womenswear, as this is the biggest fashion market sector, based on age group, life style and price bracket. In the UK, designer ranges are shown on the runway and at an exhibition during London Fashion Week; middle-market womenswear is shown at Pure in London (see Figure 4.2) and Moda UK in Birmingham exhibits menswear, womenswear, footwear and accessories. The choice of fashion trade exhibitions in the UK changes relatively frequently, with several established shows having closed their doors in recent years, with new fairs springing up to take their place. Trade fairs are usually open only to people in the fashion trade, such as buyers, designers and salespeople, but some also admit students. Tickets may be free with an invitation from an exhibitor but an admission charge is often made at the entrance. Trade magazines and websites usually

Figure 4.2 Pure womenswear trade fair at Olympia, London. Courtesy of *Drapers*.

list where and when trade fairs take place; for example *Drapers* publishes a calendar of forthcoming international fashion events.

Designer collections

Buyers for stores which stock ready-to-wear collections such as Bloomingdales in New York and Harvey Nichols in London will be invited to have seats at the runway shows in Milan, Paris, New York and London, as they are amongst the major customers for these ranges. Mass market buyers are not usually admitted to these shows but can find out what has been shown prior to the garments going into the stores via several sources. Photographs from the runway shows are featured extensively in publications such as *Collezioni*, with more limited coverage in women's fashion magazines such as *Vogue*, *Marie-Claire* and *Elle*, shortly before the garments go into stores. Websites such as firstview.com and wgsn.com also show images from the ready-to-wear collections. Fashion TV broadcasts programmes featuring runway shows 24 hours a day internationally through its satellite TV channel and website. Many buyers travel to the major fashion cities for inspiration, often accompanied by their colleagues within the buying team and designers, either from their own retailers or from their major garment suppliers. Some of the main fashion department stores and fashion districts which buyers are likely to visit are listed in Table 4.1.

The buying cycle is to a certain extent led by the fashion calendar established by the designer catwalk collections. Although all price-levels of the fashion industry employ designers, in general usage the term designer refers to

Table 4.1 Fashion department stores and fashion districts in major cities.

City	Fashion department stores	Fashion districts
London	Harrods, Harvey Nichols, Liberty, Selfridges	Bond Street, Brompton Road, Notting Hill Gate
Milan	La Rinascente	Via della Spiga, Via Montenapoleone
New York	Macys, Bloomingdales, Henri Bendel	Manhattan
Paris	Galeries Lafayette, Au Printemps, Bon Marché	Rive Gauche (Left Bank), Rue du Sevres

the most expensive end of the market. The designer ranges show catwalk collections twice annually and are divided into two major categories: *couture* and *prêt-à-porter* (ready-to-wear). Mass market buyers are not invited to attend the *couture* shows, as the garments are sold directly to the customers through the *couture* houses. The *couture* ranges developed in the late nineteenth and early twentieth centuries, hitting the peak of their influence in the 1950s. However by the end of the twentieth century their influence had declined and they are now rarely the source of widespread fashion trends, as ready-to-wear shows now have a much greater effect on fashion. The biannual fashion shows for autumn/winter and spring/summer retain the structure of two seasons per year throughout the industry despite the fact that high street retailers change their ranges more frequently.

Couture fashion shows

The term *couture* is sometimes mistakenly used as a catch-all term to describe all designer ranges but in its strictest definition *couture* ranges are limited to designers with an *atelier* (studio) based in Paris. True *couture* garments are one-offs in that they are fitted to the customer's own measurements and sewn by hand. Though several customers may own the same style of garment there is a very exclusive clientele for this type of product, limited to a few hundred people worldwide. The price of *couture* garments is often in excess of £10 000 per outfit. Although this may seem exorbitant to the mass-market fashion consumer many *couture* houses, perhaps surprisingly, fail to make a profit. This is not generally due to poor business practice as the *couture* range is the key component in the brand's promotional strategy. The laborious nature of personalised fitting and pattern amendment, expensive fabrics and trims, contribute greatly to the high price of *couture* garments. However the most significant cost is the catwalk show, which may last for only an hour, but can cost more than £100 000. Supermodels parade *couture* garments to a handpicked audience of press and customers. The costs of the fashion show can be recouped by extensive national and international press coverage which may be worth much more than spending the equivalent money on advertising. This is the conduit by which the general public, most of whom would never dream of purchasing a *couture* garment, buy into this glamorous world by purchasing spin-off products such as perfume. Licensed products, particularly accessories and toiletries, provide the bread and butter turnover of many *couture* houses, due to worldwide mass market sales. Most *couture* houses also have their own *prêt-à-porter* ranges to which the *couture* range gives added prestige.

Ready-to-wear fashion shows

Ready-to-wear refers to garments at designer level which are mass-produced, rather than fitted to the individual customer. Ready-to-wear ranges are shown separately from *couture* ranges in February and September each year, approximately six months in advance of garments being delivered to stores, with most publicity given to shows in Milan, Paris, London and New York. Ready-to-wear collections are less expensive than *couture* ranges as they are not individually fitted, but the costs of staging fashion shows, advertising and the high quality of design, pattern-cutting, fabric and manufacture result in the garments costing more than high street products. The fact that ready-to-wear garments are usually manufactured in smaller quantities than mass-market products also contributes towards the higher price bracket as this can reduce cost-effectiveness in production. However, those designers who are very successful commercially and are known internationally, such as Calvin Klein, Donna Karan and Prada can produce garments in equivalent quantities to high street retailers. It is an open secret that most high street retailers derive much of their inspiration from ready-to-wear collections. Though mass market buyers are unlikely to be able to gain access to the runway shows the ranges can be viewed prior to the season via the internet and magazines, allowing high street retailers to develop their own versions of key catwalk trends – often within the same season. A strong connection has developed between the clothes worn by celebrities and high street trends, fuelled by the launch of numerous magazines and TV programmes focusing on celebrities within the past decade.

Designer diffusion ranges for the high street

Many ready-to-wear brands produce what are known as 'diffusion' ranges, where their signature looks are applied to a cheaper version of the catwalk collections, such as DKNY (Donna Karan), CK (Calvin Klein) and Versus (Versace). These ranges can be very profitable, trading on the status and image conveyed by the brands' more expensive collections. During the 1990s, the diffusion system was extended by several British designers by producing collections in conjunction with major high street retailers and mail order companies. Marks and Spencer were at the forefront of this approach by employing designers such as Paul Smith and Betty Jackson as design consultants. Debenhams have since taken the lead, introducing ranges that are much lower in price with higher quantities than at designer level, but more expensive than the average in-house Debenhams range, including Star by Julien Macdonald and *J* by Jasper Conran. The advantages to the designers are that their work reaches a much wider audience and their fees help to finance their catwalk collections. Perhaps surprisingly, the use of such renowned designers by Marks and Spencer was not publicised initially – until the practice became widespread in other retailers – and 1999 saw the launch of the Autograph range, a higher-price-bracket collection sold in the designer-style section of a limited number of stores.

In-house design departments

Certain fashion retailers have their own design departments based at head office located near the buying department. Most retailers' design departments concentrate on compiling trend boards (also known as mood boards or storyboards), colour palettes and styling ideas for future seasons, having analysed trend forecasting information. Designers often travel with their counterparts from the buying department on directional shopping trips and visits to trade fairs, to discuss trends and design concepts at the initial planning stage. Designers for some retailers, such as Marks and Spencer, focus almost entirely on fashion forecasting and then brief designers from their manufacturers on the major trends which they have identified. Design departments in several other retailers (including Adams, Next, Oasis and Warehouse) are responsible for designing the garments which are sold in their stores.

Garment suppliers' design departments

Some retailers rely on garment suppliers for information on fashion trends, particularly when the supplier has a UK-based design team. The manufacturer's design department will be responsible for compiling trend information and suggesting garment concepts to buyers. The manufacturer's designers may compile storyboards with general trends applicable to the season to be shown to several retailers, or put together storyboards aimed at individual retailers. The design team would probably choose to show the same trend information to several retailers if their customers were in a similar age and price bracket. The design department may compile the trend boards as a team, benefiting from a wider range of ideas and research, or individual designers may work on storyboards aimed solely at the retailers for which they design. Meetings are arranged between the buyer and at least one of the designers for the garment supplier to present the storyboards, usually in the buying office, or occasionally at the supplier's premises. The manufacturer's head of design may attend this key meeting to support the designer. Having seen trend presentations from various garment suppliers the buyer will be able to form a viewpoint on the main trends which are applicable to the season and the customer.

Compiling fashion forecasting information

The various looks for a season can be shown on trend boards, which usually take the form of a professionally presented collage, filled mainly with photographs from current fashion magazines (see Figure 4.3). A great deal of thought and analysis goes into compiling a successful trend board and many images

Figure 4.3 Menswear trend board from River Island 2006. Courtesy of River Island.

are rejected before reaching the final selection. The number of themes required will probably be similar from one season to the next, so for womenswear five themes may be needed, including three new fashion trends and two classic looks. Five themes may have been selected to relate to the amount of space available in most of the retailer's stores. The fashion industry seems to have an unofficial rule that for each season there will be at least one retro and one ethnic look, and the two can often be combined. Although this may seem limiting it actually offers endless scope considering the number of historical periods and ethnic cultures from which the designer and buyer can draw inspiration.

During the late 1990s, fashion trends were highly influenced by the 1970s and Indian-style fabrics and trims. Retro looks are usually derived from at least two decades ago, so the early 1980s look which started to influence ready-to-wear fashion designers in the late 1990s has continued to be one of the main inspirations for the mass market at the beginning of the twenty-first century. Retro looks are rarely revived in exactly the same form as the original inspiration, partly because of contemporary technical innovations, such as fabric construction and new machinery. One of the reasons for a look being revived about 20 years later could be that teenagers, who are usually at the forefront of new trends, are not old enough to remember this style of clothing from the first time around. As their parents probably no longer wear this look it could be considered a subtle form of rebellion to project an image that has been discarded by an older generation. However, as fashion consumers crave more products, the internet accelerates visual communication of trends and retailers become increasingly competitive, it is likely that fashions will be revived with increasing frequency.

Presenting trend boards

A huge amount of information is available in the fashion media and the designer or buyer needs to be able to filter out those trends which are irrelevant to the customer, while focusing on those which have the highest sales potential. After observing trends on trips and in magazines, the designer will have developed ideas of working titles and the mood for the looks which are appropriate for the season. A brief written description may be compiled at this stage which could include colours, types of fabric or yarn, print ideas, garment types, silhouettes, styling details and the source of inspiration for a particular mood, such as 1950s sportswear. Images relating to these themes are collected mostly in the form of 'tear sheets' (pages torn from fashion magazines). Since many designers have access to the same fashion magazines it is also worth looking at non-fashion publications for inspiration, such as gardening, film, travel and interiors magazines, especially for colour stories, to make trend boards appear a little more original. This can improve the aesthetic appeal of the trend boards, with more variety than the ubiquitous runway poses and may therefore be more memorable to the buyers and designers who use the boards for inspiration.

Having initially collected numerous tear sheets for each story the designer goes through a selection process, being ruthless enough to discard those images which are not essential and possibly needing to seek better visuals for some of the boards. The layout of the boards, which are usually A2 or A3 size, needs to be considered simultaneously with the content and it is important to experiment with the location of the images to ensure that there is a focal point. Depending on the facilities available to the designer, the images may be scanned and manipulated using a computer program such as Adobe® Photoshop. Many designers continue to compile mood boards by hand, as this is usually quicker, and the content is generally considered to be more important than the quality of presentation in such a fast-moving industry.

Fabric swatches which are relevant to the theme can be included in trend boards (although it is not always possible to find them in appropriate colours). If fabric is included it is obviously important to consider its position in the layout either as a section containing fabrics only or as swatches dispersed across the board. It is important to present the fabrics neatly and professionally otherwise they may not sit well with the rest of the trend information. A title for each theme should be added to the board, so that each look can be referred to more easily. This is usually for the designers' and buyers' reference but may also be used to brief shop staff and can eventually find its way to the customer, for instance as a title for a section in a mail order catalogue. It is important that the title is brief and descriptive to be effective, usually three words at most.

Compiling colour palettes

A colour palette (or colour story) is a selected group of shades which are linked together to form part of a particular fashion trend. Trend boards usually contain colour palettes so that it is obvious which colours are appropriate for each theme. The colours are usually compiled either from fabric swatches or from a computer-aided design (CAD) package. The colour palettes also need to be available separately from the boards, so that they can be distributed to fabric and garment suppliers to specify colours for mass production. Colour palettes made from fabric swatches have the advantage of being easier for matching dyes, since the colour should look reasonably similar on another fabric. For colour palettes it is best to use fabrics with a fairly matt appearance and avoid fabrics with a high sheen such as satin, since the colour will vary a great deal according to the lighting conditions. (However, the reverse side of a satin fabric is usually matt and can be used successfully.) It is essential to give suppliers sufficiently large swatches as it would be difficult to dye a colour effectively from a piece of fabric the size of a postage stamp (though this has actually been known to happen). A garment manufacturer may need to request fabric to be dyed to the same shade from three different fabric suppliers as well as retaining a swatch for their own reference. For this reason it is worth the buyer ordering a sample length of at least a metre of a fabric being used in a colour palette, if the original fabric colour came from a header card from a fabric manufacturer's range. Yarns can also be included in colour palettes, particularly for knitwear ranges.

Summary

Fashion buyers are responsible for identifying future fashion trends from a variety of sources which can include:

- fashion forecasting publications and websites
- fashion trade fairs

- ready-to-wear collections
- design teams.

Trend boards may occasionally be produced by buying-teams but are more often the responsibility of the retailer's or supplier's design teams.

Further reading

Goworek, H. (2006) *Careers in Fashion and Textiles*. Blackwell Publishing, Oxford.
International Textiles
Textile View
firstview.com
ftv.com
www.wgsn.com

Chapter 5

Range Planning

Range planning involves compiling a commercially acceptable collection of garments within financial and design parameters, prior to production and delivery. The initial range plan usually takes the form of a list of appropriate garments that the buyer intends to purchase for a given season and which should cost no more than a set budget. Most stores categorise their products as 'fashion', 'basic' and 'classic' items, though they may use different terminology, such as 'contemporary' or 'core' styles. It is necessary for the buyer to gather as much information as possible regarding the past (historical sales figures), present (store visits and comparative shopping) and future (directional shopping and fashion forecasting) before planning a range. The range plan is a working document which is presented at pre-selection and final range selection meetings. The range plan is updated after the range has been finalised and then becomes a definitive list of the products to be offered for a particular season.

Compiling a range plan

The two main sources of reference for range planning are the retailer's sales figures for previous seasons and the fashion trends that have been predicted for future seasons. These two factors need to be considered within the context of the retailer's potential customers and are often based upon educated guesswork about which new trends the customers are likely to identify with. The buyer needs to be familiar with the company's size range and most stores have a variable sizing policy, with the buyer needing to decide whether certain garments should be available in smaller and/or larger size ranges. The choice of fabric for a garment and the amount of design detail included within a product greatly influence the cost, and the buyer needs to be aware of how much design content is affordable within a garment in order to keep it within the potential customer's reach. When buying a new season's range the fashion buyer needs to plan the following, some of which will be guided by the merchandise department:

- number of garments to be included in the range
- proportion of different types of garment to be included (how many tops compared to bottoms, or fashion compared to classic styles)

- specific garment styles to be included
- fabrics and colourways to be offered in each style
- cost prices for each style
- selling prices for each style
- sizes to be offered across the range and for individual styles
- which manufacturer to use for each style
- order quantities per style.

Seasons and phases

As discussed in Chapter 3, new ranges are launched for two main seasons per year. Within the spring/summer and autumn/winter seasons, buyers develop several ranges to be launched at various times and appropriate for the seasonal weather and changes in fashion trends. Because of the relatively early introduction of spring collections in most stores – actually during winter – the 'spring season' tends to be a misnomer and the buyer must ensure that the first phase of merchandise is appropriate for colder weather. The changes within a season are usually incremental with small new garment ranges introduced alongside existing stock. Most fashion multiples take delivery of spring/summer collections in January, merchandised separately from sale stock. The new ranges are usually displayed in store windows to notify customers of their arrival and to entice them into the shop.

Ranges launched at different times within the same season can be referred to as 'phases', with typically six phases per season, i.e. one per month. Within each phase, ranges may be broken down further into sub-ranges of garments which will be sold together within a particular area of a store or on the same page of a website or catalogue. For most retailers, the period from late December to mid-January is usually devoted to sales markdowns. Most trend-conscious stores launch new ranges at least every six weeks, resulting in stock being constantly updated and offering customers a very wide choice of products. This also results in the need for continuous range-planning for buyers working in this market sector. Certain product areas have distinct seasonal sales patterns, particularly those suitable for particular weather conditions such as swimwear and overcoats. With at least one overseas holiday per year becoming the norm for most customers and the increasing popularity of long-haul winter-sun holidays some stores may choose to stock a small range of swimwear throughout the year. Despite the widespread use of central heating in the UK keeping homes at a constant temperature, stores usually sell twice as much nightwear during an autumn/winter season as during a spring/summer season.

Sales history

There is much valuable information available to the buyer from the sales history of previous seasons. Patterns have probably been established of the type of fashion merchandise which the retailer's customers have purchased in the past. This sales information should be available within the buying office or from the merchandise department. Bestsellers from recent seasons need to be replaced with new yet equally profitable merchandise. It is important for the buyer to be able to judge how much, and in what ways, a bestselling style should be amended to prolong its appeal in future seasons. If the same style is offered for more than one season sales may be lower as many customers have already bought the garment, but if the style is changed substantially it may lose the appeal which made it a bestseller. The buyer needs to analyse which factors contributed towards its bestselling status – selling price and fabric are likely to be factors which can be reused from one season to the next as opposed to colour and styling which tend to be more transient qualities for fashion items.

Translating a bestselling style into the key colours for the next season and changing the buttons, trims or stitch detail could be appropriate for customers who prefer classic merchandise, the middle price bracket within the mass market. At the more fashion-conscious end of the market however the customer may expect a radically different range of garments each season with perhaps the only similarity between bestsellers from one season to the next being the price point. It is important to include a suitable proportion of new styles within each season's range whatever the market, as bestselling styles inevitably have a limited life cycle (see Chapter 11) and some innovations will eventually become bestsellers. If garments have not sold well, it is important to establish the reasons for this in order to avoid the same problem arising in future seasons. This is often easier to establish in mail order companies, as customers are requested to give reasons for returns (see Chapter 9). It is important that retail buyers visit stores to discover reasons for poor garment sales, as sales staff can provide a wealth of information about customer feedback (see Chapter 11). However, not all stores are typical: London's Oxford Street, for example, contains many retailers' flagship stores, but the customer mix is biased towards tourists.

Directional and comparative shopping

During directional shopping trips several key garments are usually bought in a standard size so that they can be fitted on a model back at head office, and some of the measurements may be used for specifications for the retailer's own styles. The samples may also be bought for colour or fabric reference and could end up being cut into swatches for next season's colour palette. Intellectual property laws mean it is illegal to copy someone else's design. However this does take place within the fashion industry and though it often happens without legal repercussions there have been cases where the originators of garment designs have successfully sued companies who have plagiarised their ideas. There is a myth within the industry that it is acceptable to copy a design if a certain number of elements are changed. This, according to Mark Hurley,

Director of Intellectual Property at De Montfort University, is untrue (personal communication). The law of copyright applies automatically to fashion designs but it can be difficult to clarify at which point copyright is infringed by a style which is similar to the original. There can be little doubt however that producing style with the same colour, fabric type, silhouette and design details as another could result in a company being sued. Many examples of litigation regarding copying fashion styles are reported in the press, and this appears to have increased since the rise of 'fast fashion' ranges.

Options and colourways

The number of garment styles in the range including each colourway on offer is referred to as the number of options (or ways). In the range plan in Table 5.1, for example, there are seven garment styles with a total of twelve options. After initially planning the range the buyer should check it again to avoid duplication in terms of price, colour, style and fabric. If two styles are very similar to each other, for instance two red shirts at the same selling price, this can result in one style taking sales from the other. It is therefore advisable to differentiate styles in order to maximise the amount that customers want to buy. If, however, a red shirt were viewed as the season's must-have garment, it would be beneficial to offer more than one within a range; offering two at different prices in different fabrics could help to increase rather than split sales.

The ratio of tops to bottoms is a key factor in the planning of a succesful range. Generally more tops than bottoms should be offered as tops tend to be cheaper, and therefore the customer is likely to buy more tops than trousers or skirts. It is possible to achieve this by offering tops in a wider variety of colourways than the rest of the range, or by increasing the number of styles of top. When buying ranges of lingerie the opposite approach should be taken as customers usually buy more briefs than bras. The lingerie buyer may choose to include the same number of briefs as bra styles within the range or even buy more bra styles, but the briefs could be offered in packs of three or five pairs.

Sizing

The selected range of sizes in which garments are available can vary between retailers, and between ranges within a store. The standard size range is 10–16 in the UK. A choice of only four sizes can be restrictive for consumers, and many stores stock from size 8 to size 18 with smaller sizes such as 6 considered to be 'petite', and size 20 and over often termed 'outsize'. Whilst petite could be considered a flattering term outsize has negative connotations for many potential customers and should therefore be avoided. The Arcadia Group's Evans chain wisely dropped 'Outsize' from its name during the 1980s and has capitalised on its position as the UK's major retailer focusing on size 16 and

Table 5.1 Example of a range plan.

WOMENSWEAR RANGE PLAN. Season: spring/summer 2008, high summer. Product area: jerseywear

Reference number	Product description	Supplier	Colourways	Fabric quality	Size range	Cost price	Selling price
SS091	Short-sleeved T-shirt with gathered neckline	VS Garments, Turkey	Raspberry Mango	97% cotton 3% lycra jersey	8–20	£4.07	£12
SS092	Strappy vest	VS Garments, Turkey	Raspberry Mango Sage	100% cotton 1 × 1 rib	8–16	£2.58	£8
SS093	Long-sleeved round-neck top with embroidered logo	Quality Style Ltd., China	Mango Sage	100% cotton needle-out interlock	8–20	£5.89	£18
SS094	V-neck fitted cardigan with trimmed neckline	Quality Style Ltd., China	Raspberry	1 × 1 rib	8–20	£6.45	£20
SS095	Lightweight hooded fleece with zip and embroidered logo	Quality Style Ltd., China	Raspberry Sage	100% polyester fleece	S M L	£6.34	£20
SS096	Shorts with drawstring waist and embroidered logo on pocket	Afyon Clothing, Turkey	Raspberry	98% cotton 2% lycra single jersey	8–16	£4.96	£15
SS097	Trouser with rib waistband	Afyon Clothing, Turkey	Mango	100% cotton interlock waistband 1 × 1 rib	8–20	£6.72	£20

above, including ranges by designers such as Sonja Nuttall. Women's figures are notoriously variable, and it is therefore advisable to sell suits as separate items as it is often the case that a woman who wears a size 16 skirt may take a size 14 in a top.

During the late 1990s, several high street stores realised the sales potential of extending their size ranges. A strategy of offering the same clothes as the standard size range in larger and smaller sizes appealed to customers as it stopped them from being marked out as different by being excluded from mainstream trends. Until the mid-1990s many major store chains in the UK preferred not to stock larger sizes, partly because it was viewed as less prestigious but also because ordering more sizes could be more complex and less economical because of higher fabric usage. As fashion retailing becomes increasingly competitive buyers constantly seek ways to stay ahead of the field and the decision about which sizes to stock can be a critical factor in the success of a range.

Fashion buyers need to review which sizes to offer in complete garment ranges or individual styles. This decision can be based on an in-depth examination of sales per size for past season's range, giving the buyer sufficient information to decide whether a new garment with a similar fit to a previous one should be offered in the same size range. The buyer may choose to seek advice from the QC department to establish a suitable size range for a garment. The overall range of sizes offered by a retailer will probably be a senior management decision and the buyer is permitted to select size ranges per garment within these parameters. It is a good idea for the buying manager to oversee the sizing policy of several buyers' ranges as customers will probably choose to put garments from different buyers' ranges within a store together as outfits, and offering one range up to size 18 and another up to size 24 under exactly the same label would give out a confusing message. Some retailers make a conscious decision to give a different label and image to ranges aimed at particular size ranges, like the 'Précis' petite range at Debenhams.

In the UK, size 12 garments, the industry's accepted standard size for womenswear samples, are shown at range selection meetings. Garments are fitted on models to achieve the correct cut and proportion before the style is graded into the full size range. Size 12 is selected as it is usually one of the middle sizes in a range and presents less risk of problems of fit being magnified. (A buyer who is a standard size 12 will probably be in demand for fitting sessions, but this unfortunate addition to the workload can be outweighed by the occasional perk of a free sample or wearer trial.) For menswear, size 42 is used for standard fittings and, for a childrenswear range from 2–10, size 7–8 is often used for samples. Women's shoes are usually sampled in a size 4, and men's in a size 10.

Sizing usually varies in measurement from one retailer to another, as most consumers will know from experience. This is because there is no fashion industry standard for sizing and the fit of the garment can be part of its style. There are British Standards for sizes based on the measurements of the body but most garments are obviously not required to be skin tight and need to be bigger than the body to allow enough room for the wearer to move comfortably. A retailer's QC department usually sets the precise measurements for each garment size, including bust, waist, hips and many more detailed dimensions, such as nape of the neck to the waist and sleeve lengths.

Calculating retail prices

It would probably come as a shock to most high street customers to find that many retailers in the UK charge the customer 2.5 to 3.5 times more than the price the manufacturer charged them for a garment. This is not pure profit for the retailer as the vast majority, and sometimes all, of this amount is spent on overheads such as store rents, rates, electricity, head office costs and staffing (including buyers' salaries). The full target margin also takes into account that a certain percentage of merchandise will inevitably be marked down.

Each company has its own target margin and a set formula for achieving it. Calculating the formula will become second nature to a buyer after a few weeks or months working for a retailer. It is important for fashion buyers to be numerate to a certain level as there is a reasonable amount of mathematics involved in the job, but the same basic calculations tend to be repeated frequently, and it is not necessary to have a deep knowledge of mathematics. The merchandiser's job usually requires a higher level of numeracy than buying, although it is usual for American buyers to have much more involvement with figures than their counterparts in the UK.

The price paid by the retailer to the manufacturer for a garment is known as the 'cost price', which is explained in more detail in Chapter 7. At the final range selection meeting buyers suggest retail selling prices for the garments; this is the amount that will be charged for the product in the store based on the cost price from the supplier, the retailer's target mark-up (or margin) and the price that the buyer anticipates the customer will be prepared to pay. If the retailer's target selling price is three times the cost price the buyer generally uses this calculation as the starting point, rounded up to the nearest pound. The buyer has to estimate the price that the customer will be prepared to pay, based on previous experience, whilst gaining a suitable profit margin for the company.

It has become conventional for many stores in the UK to round up prices to the nearest 99 pence. This practice started after decimalisation in the 1970s, with the idea that it appealed psychologically to the customer. Since the 1990s however the trend has been for fashion stores at higher price levels to sell garments priced in exact pounds, possibly because the .99p price tag has become associated with cheapness and the lower end of the market. Where clothing is concerned it is unusual for stores to use prices ending in random figures apart from the occasional .49p or .50p. Some stores combine both pricing methods, occasionally using the .99p price tag for their cheaper merchandise.

Most buyers calculate the margin based on the following principle:

$$\frac{\text{selling price} - \text{cost price}}{\text{selling price}} \times 100 = \text{margin percentage}$$

The examples below are for a retailer with a mark-up of around three times cost price:

(a) Selling price = £30; cost price = £10

$$\frac{(30 - 10)}{30} \times 100 = 66.67\%$$

(b) Selling price = £45; cost price = £14

$$\frac{(45 - 14)}{45} \times 100 = 68.89\%$$

Margins are usually expressed as percentages rounded up to two decimal places. Example (a) demonstrates that a mark-up of exactly three times the cost price results in a percentage margin of 66.67%, which would be the retailer's target margin. Example (b) shows that if the cost price is lower than a third of the selling price, then the percentage margin is higher (and therefore more profitable). Each retailer has its own formula for calculating retail prices, accounting for factors such as Value Added Tax (VAT) in the UK at a rate of 17.5%. The formula for each company is confidential and is likely to be a little more complex than the examples above, but new recruits to the company will obviously be given access to it. Many buyers initially have the formula taped onto a calculator, until they have memorised it, and the computer software used by most retailers can automatically calculate margins. Childrenswear is not eligible for VAT so the formula will vary a little, but as some teenagers' garments have the same dimensions as adult clothing, VAT may have to be included. Larger children's clothes require more material and this, as well as VAT, accounts for the increase in prices in children's garments and footwear in the older age ranges.

The examples in Table 5.2 show how to calculate retail selling prices from cost prices, based on a store which has a mark-up of three times the cost price.

Table 5.2 Setting retail selling prices.

Garment description	Manufacturer's cost price	Cost price × 3	Rounded up/down to nearest pound	Final retail selling price and margin
Girls' red jersey shirt with embroidered detail	£3.28	£9.84	£10	£12 (72.67%)
Girls' indigo denim jeans	£8.42	£25.26	£25	£25 (66.32%)

In example (1) in Table 5.2, the red jersey shirt would meet the company's target profit margin if it were sold at £10, but the buyer has decided that a selling price of £12 is more appropriate, as the embroidered logo makes it more desirable to the customer than a competitor's plain shirt which retails at £9. This selling price has the bonus of giving the retailer a higher profit. In example (2) the buyer has decided to maintain the retail selling price at £25 despite being slightly less than three times the cost price, as this is the same price charged by a direct competitor, and charging £26 could result in customers deciding to shop elsewhere. The buyer would probably have to gain approval from the buying manager for the margin on the jeans as it is slightly below the target. The buying manager would look at this in the context of the whole range, taking into account that the high margin on the red shirt would help to compensate, depending on the quantities ordered for each of the two styles.

After range planning buyers in some companies are expected to calculate the average margin, average selling price and average cost price of the range in order to anticipate the expected margins and consequent profits. The principle of calculating the average margin is relatively simple but it depends on entering data on every style in the range accurately and this demands a great deal of preparation. The average selling price is initially calculated by adding together the selling price of every option in the range and dividing it by the total number of options in the range.

In the range plan shown previously in Table 5.1, there are seven styles with a total of 12 options, accounting for the various colourways. The average selling price can be calculated as follows:

$$(£8 \times 3) + (£12 \times 2) + £15 + (£18 \times 2) + (£20 \times 4) = £179 \div 12 \text{ options} = £14.92$$

A range plan usually includes a far greater number of styles, and it is therefore important to recheck the figures as mistakes can easily occur. The average selling price is further affected by the quantities ordered per style, since a low selling price on a high volume style could have an adverse affect. Retailers may therefore prefer to factor order quantities into the average selling price. Average selling prices however are usually calculated at the range selection stage before order quantities are finalised, to assess the overall performance of the range. Buyers at a final range selection meeting may also be asked how the average selling price compares with that of previous seasons, and a distinct increase in average selling price would need to be justified.

This may seem like an exercise more suited to an accountant but it is very much part of planning a financially successful range. By doing this the buyer can identify which garments are not making enough profit margin and take the opportunity to replace such styles before placing orders with manufacturers. This type of calculation would usually be undertaken by buyers at a senior level using a computer program such as a specialist spreadsheet, so is not as daunting or complicated as might first appear. By calculating the average margin of the range the buyer may be able to include garments which do not appear to be sufficiently profitable but are compensated for by higher margins from other garments.

Classifying fashion merchandise within the range plan

In order to achieve a balanced offer of merchandise within any fashion range the buyer needs to achieve the right mix between classic and fashionable products. Some retailers recognise this by having different buyers for classic and fashionable styles rather than dividing the range by garment types.

Classic, core and basic products

Some retailers retain classic products within a range for more than one season either in exactly the same form or by retaining the styling and amending the colour or fabric. This often applies to menswear and even image-conscious chains like Gap sell basic trouser styles for two or more seasons in classic colours such as stone, while introducing more fashionable colours on a seasonal basis. For womenswear, classic products tend to be sold mostly at a mass market level with stores such as Bhs selling a proportion of classic styles which evolve slightly from year to year alongside shorter-term fashion merchandise.

Lingerie tends to have a longer life cycle than other clothing items with classic styles being produced for several years because underwear is usually concealed, thereby reducing the peer pressure to wear the latest styles and colours. This may not be true however for fashion retailers with a young customer profile, as certain types of underwear are worn to be seen.

Even at the younger end of the market there are classic products which vary only slightly in styling from one season to the next including jeans and T-shirts. Classic products tend to achieve their status by combining comfort and practicality with aesthetic appeal, like riding boots. Classic products can achieve a relatively long product life cycle (see Chapter 11) lasting several years, compared with most fashion items which are usually stocked for a maximum of six months. Classic colours usually include black, navy, cream and white, but can vary from one product area or market level to another. For lingerie white is a classic and consistently bestselling colour with white bras outselling every other colour put together in many underwear ranges. Depending on the retailer, classic products are also referred to as 'core' or 'basic' merchandise.

Fashion products and fads

Most clothing or footwear products which are considered to be fashionable items are stocked by retailers for no longer than one season. A minority of fashion products go on to become classic items. An item may be stocked as a fashion product by one retailer, yet another store aimed at a younger, more fashion-conscious customer may include a similar garment in its basic range. A fad is a very short-term fashion, but one which achieves high sales figures within that period. Fads tend to be adopted more by younger customers at the cheaper end of the market, the style's popularity often being fuelled by media interest. The item's high profile may have been prompted by press coverage of a celebrity wearing a designer item: for example the dominance of gypsy skirts and large leather belts in the high street in 2005 has been attributed to widespread press coverage at the time of the actress Sienna Miller. The buyer needs to use experience and instinct to identify whether a style is a fad or a longer-term fashion item in order to estimate how long a product should be kept in the range.

Factors which affect the performance of a fashion range

There are numerous factors which affect range planning and the subsequent commercial success of a fashion range. The buyer is usually the main focus for the performance of the range but retailers recognise that it is not possible for an individual to control all of the internal and external factors which have an impact upon range planning and sales figures.

Internal factors

Below are some of the internal factors within a retailer which can influence range planning:

- promotion, e.g. TV advertisements or window displays
- available budget
- the company's buying policy
- takeover/acquisition
- the performance of the company's other departments, e.g. merchandising, QC, sales
- management decisions
- company restructuring.

Armed with a thorough knowledge of sales history, customers, competitors' ranges and trends, the buyer has a better opportunity of buying a commercially successful range. The buyer needs to work within the constraints applied by the internal factors listed above and if, for example, the company's available buying budget has been used in another product area a buyer may be unable to make mid-season purchases of the latest fashion items, thus losing potential sales.

Most companies' promotional strategies involve photographing key items to be displayed as in-store advertising or on the cover of a catalogue. This can have a profound effect on the sales of the chosen styles, which needs to be anticipated when specifying order quantities. A retailer's buying policy inevitably affects the success of its ranges so if, for example, buyers are permitted to buy only from certain countries they may miss out on manufacturing techniques and styling details available in other countries. The takeover of a company is also likely to result in a change in the retailer's buying policy.

The way in which the other key departments at head office operate is crucial to the success of a range as the development of fashion products is undoubtedly a team effort. Sales staff also play a key role as they can influence the customer's purchase decision in-store. Management decisions can overrule a buyer's plans, but can equally be of great support. The restructuring of a buying team inevitably affects the way in which a range is bought as, for example, merging two product areas under one buyer could potentially be a positive move to give more synergy to the range providing this change is backed up by sufficient support and assistance within the team.

External factors

However effectively the company operates internally many external factors can also contribute to the performance of a range, including:

- current social and fashion trends
- economic factors
- ranges on offer from competitors
- customer buying decisions
- supplier performance
- weather.

If there is a downturn in the economy retailers can expect sales to be less buoyant and sales figures need to be analysed in the context of the performance of the fashion sector as a whole. If competitors introduce innovations in the product area they could take away sales from other retailers. Customer buying decisions are obviously vital to the success of a range and during the interiors and DIY boom of the late 1990s, driven by the proliferation of TV programmes of this genre, many consumers chose to direct their disposable income into this area in preference to clothing. The performance of suppliers, particularly in terms of quality and deliveries, clearly has a profound effect on a fashion range, and the buyer's reliance on manufacturers was explained earlier. The weather often has a major impact on sales of fashion items and whilst the buyer can foresee certain changes of temperature throughout the year the UK climate in particular is notoriously unpredictable. Fashion sales can be affected directly by customers purchasing items suitable for the current weather but there can be a more profound effect in extreme conditions, such as the widespread floods in 2000, which, combined with the repair of the UK national rail network at the same time, resulted in clothes shopping becoming a low priority if not impractical for many consumers. There is usually very little that the buyer can do to influence external factors such as those listed above but, by remaining aware of the market as a whole as well as social trends, their effects can at least be anticipated.

Summary

Range planning involves specifying the details of a fashion range at least once per season season including:

- style, fabric and colour details
- cost prices and selling prices
- manufacturers
- sizes
- order quantities.

Within the range, products can be classified as fashion or classic merchandise. A variety of internal and external factors affect range planning and the subsequent performance of the range.

Chapter 6

Fabric Sourcing

Fabric sourcing can sometimes be part of the buyer's job when a fashion range is developed exclusively for a retailer's own stores. This may be done in association with designers, fabric technologists and garment manufacturers. Buyers of own-label ranges are becoming less involved in fabric sourcing now that such a high proportion of products are manufactured overseas, relying instead on garment suppliers to do this for them. Buyers for independent stores who select from branded ranges are never involved in fabric sourcing; this reduces the workload but does not give the buyer the option of selecting fabrics. Buyers for knitwear source yarn rather than fabrics and there are specific trade fairs for yarn suppliers. Buyers are not expected to be technical experts on fabrics but some knowledge of the terminology and appearance of fabrics is very useful as buyers are responsible for investing large sums of the company's money in textiles. Buyers are continually learning about fabrics as the industry is constantly developing innovations and reviving traditional fabrics. It is a good idea for buyers to visit fabric manufacturers to view production if time permits as this gives them an idea of the production constraints.

Fibre content

All fabrics are manufactured from either natural or synthetic fibres. It is important to differentiate between the fibre content and the construction as they are two distinctly separate attributes of a fabric. The fibre content is included on a garment's label stating what the fabric was made from but it does not offer any information about how the fabric itself was constructed. A single type of fibre such as cotton can be constructed into many fabric forms, from a lightweight stretch knitted single jersey to a heavyweight woven cloth such as denim.

Natural fibres

Natural fibres are derived directly from either plant or animal sources. Cotton, hemp, linen and ramie are examples of fibres originating from plants whereas wool, angora, cashmere, mohair and silk are derived from animals. Fabrics containing natural fibres are often viewed as more luxurious than synthetics, with the possible exception of cotton, which is the most widely-used natural fibre.

Synthetic fibres

Synthetic fibres are man-made, either from oil and coal derivatives, or regenerated fibres. Oil-based fibres include polyester, polyamide (nylon), acrylic and elastane. Man-made regenerated fibres are created by the chemical treatment of wood pulp, resulting in the development of acetate, tencel and viscose. Elastane fibre (also known by the trade name of Lycra® from the manufacturer Du Pont) has excellent stretch and recovery properties and is based on polyurethane. Elastane is always combined with other yarns and is never used as a fabric on its own; it can form up to 20% of the total fibre content of a fabric, depending upon the amount of stretch required. A high elastane content, such as 20%, is used mainly in swimwear and performance sportswear, often blended with polyamide or nylon. A smaller percentage, such as 2%, can be used in cotton jersey for underwear to help maintain the garment's shape during and after wear. Elastane usually costs more than the other fibres within a fabric so its inclusion can increase the price but improve the quality.

Fabric construction

Fabrics fall into two main categories of construction, knitted or woven. Knitted fabrics always have stretch properties. Fabrics can either be woven on looms or knitted on warp or weft knitting machines. There are also non-woven fabrics, though these are generally used for interlinings, which are concealed within structured garments. Until recently it has been easy to define the type of construction of a fabric because of the rigidity of woven fabrics. However the introduction of elastane into many woven fabrics gives them the capacity to stretch. To tell whether or not a stretch fabric is woven it is necessary to look closely at the weave and pull the fabric both horizontally and vertically, as the elastane usually only offers stretch in one direction. Despite the extra cost the inclusion of elastane in woven fabrics has become extremely popular because of the comfort, ease of movement and improved fit which it offers the wearer.

Woven fabrics

Woven fabrics can be identified by the warp threads which run down the length of the cloth and the weft threads which run across the width. There are many variations on woven fabric construction from basic weaves and twills such as denim to more complex weaves such as piqué, crêpe and satin. Designs can be woven into fabrics including colour wovens, such as tartans, where alternating yarn colours in the warp and weft creates a pattern, and damasks, where the pattern is self-coloured. It is possible to make a particular type of fabric from a variety of different fibres either individually or blended together.

Equally, most fibres can be used in several types of fabric construction. Some fibres lend themselves particularly well to certain fabric constructions many of which have become classic fabrics such as silk satin, to the extent that the fibre and construction can sometimes be confused with each other. Silk is a versatile fibre which can have many different appearances in fabric from shiny satin to the duller sheen of habutai. Satin can also be made in synthetic fibres, such as polyester or viscose which maintain the high sheen qualities of the fabric and can only be differentiated from silk upon close inspection.

Knitted fabrics

Knitted fabrics take the form of interlacing loops of yarn and are often referred to as jersey. Jersey can be made in a variety of constructions including interlock, rib and piqué. Jersey fabrics have differing amounts of stretch within them depending on the yarn and construction. Knitted fabrics are cut out and sewn together to make jerseywear products. Knitwear, however, is manufactured by knitting panels of garments with finished edges to specific dimensions and sewing together only the seams.

Fabric printing

Printing is one of the most popular methods of decorating fabrics, and can be a very cost-effective way of adding interest to a garment. Print designs are often taken from the fabric manufacturer's own range and are usually designed either by their own in-house textile designers or bought from freelance designers. Print designs can be all-over prints, border prints (down the selvedges of the fabric) or placement prints (designed to be put in a specific location on a garment). When the same print is available in garment ranges from two entirely separate retailers this is because they have been selected from the same fabric manufacturer's range.

A buyer can make a print design exclusive to a particular retailer in two different ways. First, if the buyer can guarantee a large order at an early stage or is a regular customer the fabric manufacturer may agree to 'confine' a print to this retailer, meaning that it will not be offered to anyone else. The agreement to confine a print usually lasts for up to a year, after which time it may become available to other retailers. Buyers also have automatic exclusivity for a print if they provide the fabric manufacturer with the design, either from an in-house team or a freelance designer. In this case the fabric manufacturer has the screens cut for this print and the costs incurred will probably be added to the price of the fabric per metre, sometimes making it more expensive than a fabric in the supplier's own range. As a compromise a buyer can gain a certain level of exclusivity on a print by requesting a particular colourway to be specially produced in an existing print from the fabric manufacturer. This could include several colours matched to the retailer's colour palette to co-ordinate with the rest of the range.

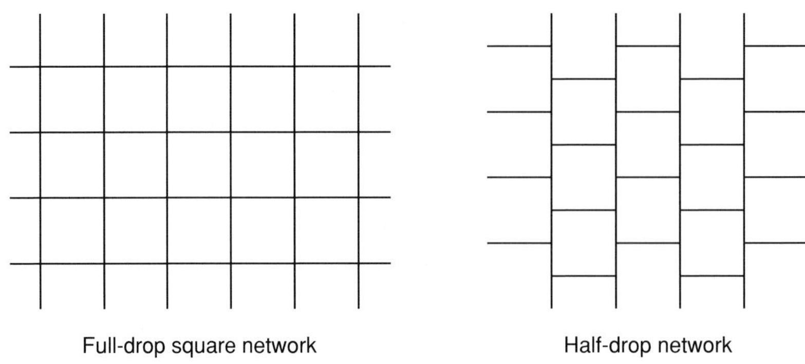

Figure 6.1 Repeat networks for fabric prints.

All-over prints

This is the standard way of printing on a fabric. The fabric is printed in repeat, meaning that it is designed in such a way that it appears to be continuous. When a printed fabric is inspected closely it should be possible to identify the size of the repeat, which is often rectangular in shape, showing where the design starts and finishes. Some textile designers produce their original designs in repeat but others use CAD software to put a design into repeat. Some printing companies employ people who specialise in doing this. It is possible to use various sizes and types of repeat for prints, including half-drop repeats, as shown in Figure 6.1.

There are several different methods of printing fabrics all over, in terms of the equipment and dye used. The most popular method is screen printing, usually involving the use of a rotary screen. The design of the print is inscribed on the rotary screen in the form of minute holes, the screen is rolled onto the fabric and ink containing dye of the specified colour is squeezed through. Each colour in a print requires one screen to be made, so the more colours there are in a print the more expensive it usually is, owing to the cost of making the screens.

Another method – transfer printing – involves printing a design onto a long roll of paper, and is particularly suitable for use on polyester fabrics. The print is applied at a high temperature and pressure by feeding the fabric and paper through rollers. This is one of the cheapest printing methods but the colours can lack intensity. Transfer printed fabric has the advantage of being relatively quick to produce if the buyer chooses prints and fabrics which are available in stock rather than developing a specific print in the retailer's own colourway.

One-way, two-way and border prints

Some types of print design are more expensive than others owing to less economical use of the fabric and therefore higher fabric wastage. Most print designs are two-way, which means that they look the same when the fabric is held upside down. When a garment is being cut out in a clothing factory each piece can be positioned either way up, allowing as much fabric as possible to be utilised with the minimum of wastage. Some print designs are one-way, meaning that the design can only be viewed from one direction, and all pieces of the garment must be cut in the same direction with less opportunity to fit in pieces economically. Consequently garments made in a one-way printed fabric can be relatively expensive as they use more fabric than a two-way print.

Border prints are similar in most respects to all-over prints in terms of printing methods. When garments are manufactured border prints are usually located at the hem or cuff, so fabric wastage can also be high using this type of design as it is hard to make economical use of every piece of fabric. It is useful for buyers to be aware of this so that they understand why garment manufacturers charge higher prices for garments with a one-way or border print.

Placement prints

As the name suggests, placement prints are placed on a specified area within a garment. This always takes place after fabric production, either directly onto a completed garment or onto a piece of fabric which has been cut out before the garment is manufactured. The advantage of placement printing before garments have been made is that it is easier to transport garment panels to the printer and to place them under the printing screens than print finished garments. Placement printing is particularly popular on T-shirts, and it is possible to keep stock of plain garments to have placement prints applied relatively quickly.

Fabric dyeing, finishing and embellishment

It is possible to dye fabrics at various stages of production. The most frequent method used is to dye fabric after it has been manufactured to a shade which a buyer has specified for a garment order. Fabric manufacturers often produce fabric in its undyed, unbleached state, which is referred to as 'greige' cloth, to be kept in stock, ready to be dyed when necessary. In yarn-dyed fabrics the yarn is dyed before it is woven or knitted. Yarn-dyed jersey fabrics include *marls,* where the yarn is dyed in shades of the same colour, resulting in a patchy effect on the fabric, and *space dyes,* where the yarn is dyed in various colours giving the fabric consecutive rows of changing shades. It is possible to dye garments after they have been manufactured, depending upon the fibre content. This can cause shrinkage to the fabric and therefore the garment, so the measurements of the garment patterns need to be increased to account for this. Garment dyeing techniques include dip-dyeing, which gives the effect of a graduation of colour, with more intense colour at the hem, fading out towards the top of the garment, or vice versa. Tie-dyeing, where parts of the garment are tied up with thread before dyeing and removed afterwards leaves circles or stripes in the original fabric colour, where the thread has resisted the dye.

Finishing techniques are applied after fabrics have been woven or knitted; jersey fabrics can be brushed to give a soft, fluffy texture, and jeans can be stonewashed after they have been manufactured to give an aged appearance. Fabrics or garments can be decorated with embellishments such as embroidery, sequins or beading. Embroidery machines can be used in mass production but beading is often applied by hand, and its labour-intensive nature means it is usually produced in the Far East or India.

Methods of fabric sourcing

Buyers for fashion multiples may see representatives from fabric manufacturers on a regular basis. It is therefore important to forge positive relationships as both parties have the aim of selling as much of their product as possible by developing products which appeal to the retailer's consumers. Fashion buyers view fabric ranges at a meeting with a sales representative or agent for the fabric company either at the retailer's office, a fabric manufacturer's or agent's showroom or at a trade fair. The buyer looks through a collection of swatches from the fabric manufacturer's range and selects those which are most appropriate for the intended season and garment range. The buyer orders fabric swatches and possibly some sample lengths of fabric. Most fashion designers working for garment manufacturers operate in the same way, selecting fabric swatches which are appropriate for the retailers for whom they design products.

Sales representatives and agents for fabric companies

The people responsible for selling fabric manufacturers' products can be employed as sales representatives directly by the company or can be self-employed, operating as agents. The sales representative is usually paid a salary by the fabric manufacturer plus a small percentage of sales turnover as a bonus. Sales agents usually work on commission only, relying solely on a percentage of the turnover for the fabric they sell for income. The agent therefore has even more sales incentive than someone employed by the company, with less job security but high earning potential, and probably sells ranges from several different fabric suppliers. Fabric companies usually employ sales representatives in their home countries but overseas rely on sales agents who are more familiar with the local market. A sales agent may be responsible for sales within several countries, for example northern Europe, a single country, or a region within a country.

Fabric merchants

Another method of buying fabric is via fabric merchants, which tend to be based in either London or the North-West, though this type of business has become threatened by the rapid reduction in UK garment manufacture. The fabric merchant does not manufacture fabric but imports it in large quantities from fabric suppliers and therefore has the buying power to negotiate discounts. The merchant operates as a middle-man by keeping fabric in stock in a warehouse to be purchased by garment manufacturers. Whaleys is one of the most established merchants in the UK, which can supply a wide selection of cloths in varying quantities (www.whaleys-bradford.ltd.uk). The garment supplier can expect to pay more per metre from the fabric merchant than purchasing the fabric directly from the manufacturer but there are usually no minimum order quantities, as the fabric has already been made and it can also be delivered very quickly. This is very important for young fashion garments as it can save months of fabric production in the Far East, the original source of a high proportion of merchants' cloth. Some fabric merchants specialise in importing base cloths, which can then be printed in Europe in a relatively short time to a design of the retailer's choice. In the fast-moving fashion business this is an important service for European garment manufacturers, as time can be more important than money in terms of missing out on a major trend.

Alternative methods of fabric sourcing

Sometimes buyers need to source a particular type of fabric during a season, and contact potential fabric suppliers by phone or email, or send swatches in the post for reference. Occasionally it is possible to find the right fabric very quickly, especially if the buyer is very experienced and is familiar with an extensive range of fabric suppliers. However this situation can often be like looking for a needle in a haystack and there are several methods that the buyer can use to speed up the process.

Contacting garment manufacturers can be quicker than contacting fabric suppliers directly as their design teams probably view a wider range of fabrics more frequently than buyers. However this may not be appropriate if the buyer wishes to place the order for the garments in this fabric with a different clothing manufacturer. Colleagues within the buying department should be asked for their advice even if they are not in the same product area, as they may have prior knowledge of sources of this fabric type. At trade fairs it is worth investing in a catalogue which lists all of the exhibitors, often classified by fabric types. There is usually a contact in the catalogue for the country in which the retailer is based. Fabric and trim suppliers often have their own websites, so the buyer can source fabrics on the internet. There are also specialist fashion websites with resource directories, such as wgsn.com, which list suppliers of both garment and fabric types. The internet provides many advantages for fabric sourcing in this global industry, and the capacity to search worldwide for a fabric without the need for numerous conversations can be very helpful to the busy fashion buyer.

Fabric and yarn trade fairs

The major European fabric exhibition is *Première Vision* (PV) in France which is held twice a year, usually in February and September (see also Chapter 3).

Texworld, held in Paris at the same time as PV, has become established as a fabric trade fair specialising in non-European textiles and has expanded to accommodate 678 exhibitors from 40 countries, with almost 19 000 visitors in September 2006. Yarn fairs such as *Expofil* are aimed primarily at the knitwear trade and take place earlier than fabric fairs as knitwear tends to have a longer product development cycle.

Trade fairs offer a centralised colour, yarn and fabric trend area, as well as numerous exhibitors showing their companies' new ranges on individual stands. PV is such a large exhibition, with hundreds of stands, that visitors need to plan a strategy to be able to target the most relevant fabric ranges. A visit to the central trend area helps the buyer to identify interesting fabrics, which are labelled with the suppliers' names. It is often necessary to make an appointment to view a range on the fabric supplier's stand as there can often be a waiting list, and many buyers organise this in advance of the trip. Sales representatives show buyers and designers new collections of fabrics from which swatches and sample lengths can be ordered (see Figure 6.2). Because of the volume of visitors to a trade fair it may take a few weeks before the swatches and samples are delivered so buyers may be permitted to cut small pieces of fabric to keep alongside details on price and fabric composition. For this reason it is always advisable to take a pair of scissors, a stapler and some fabric sourcing sheets to a trade fair (see Figure 6.3). Few fabric suppliers are likely to have time available at a trade fair to allow students to see ranges, but a visit to the show before graduation can still be beneficial.

Figure 6.2 Buyers viewing swatches on a fabric manufacturer's stand at *Première Vision*. Courtesy of *Première Vision*.

SUPPLIER			SEASON		Date
FABRIC REFERENCE Name/ number	SWATCH	PRICE per metre (CIF or FOB) and WIDTH	MINIMUM ORDER QUANTITY	DELIVERY LEAD TIME	SAMPLE QUANTITY ORDERED

Figure 6.3 Fabric sourcing sheet.

Sampling, minimums and delivery lead times

Fabric manufacturers usually produce fabric to order for customers rather than keeping it in stock, as this is more economical. A relatively short production run such as 100 metres is produced initially to make swatches and sample lengths from which to sell the fabric. Swatches are small cuttings of fabric several centimetres wide which are usually attached to a cardboard hanger or 'header', and may include the same print in several different colourways. Headers also provide vital information, such as reference numbers, percentages of fibre content, the supplier's name and suggested washing instructions. The price is not usually included, as this can vary depending on exchange rates and order quantities, and can be negotiable. After a fashion buyer or designer has viewed a fabric range, headers of fabrics which are considered to be suitable for the potential customer are requested. It is important to remember when choosing fabric swatches that the selection must be appropriate for the retailer's customer base rather than being based on the buyer's own taste. Although the swatches are relatively expensive to produce the fabric manufacturer sends them without charge to companies within the fashion industry as this is their prime method of marketing. Charging companies for swatches could deter buyers from using certain fabric suppliers.

Sample lengths are small amounts of fabric ordered by fashion buyers or designers of 1 to 10 metres which can be used to make a sample garment. The garment is often produced by a sample machinist in the manufacturer's design room and can be used in retailers' pre-selection and final range selection meetings. Companies are charged for sample lengths at the same standard price per metre as in bulk production. This is not cost-effective for the fabric manufacturer but is worthwhile as once a sample length is ordered there is a strong chance that thousands of metres could be ordered in bulk production. It is also possible to apply a CAD print from computer software directly onto a sample length of fabric using a Stork printer. This can be a very quick method of printing for samples, though the printers are relatively expensive. When viewing fabric ranges, buyers in some companies use forms such as the one in Figure 6.3 for reference relating to fabric swatches and sample lengths which they have ordered. This allows them to keep all the key details mentioned in this section as a reminder at a later date, for example to chase up delivery of a fabric which is needed for a sample garment. The representative from the fabric supplier also usually keeps a record of the sample order and gives a duplicate copy to the buyer.

When a fabric has been selected for inclusion in a retailer's garment range a bulk order is placed with the fabric supplier, usually by the garment manufacturer, after receiving a garment order from the retailer. The fabric manufacturer has a minimum order quantity below which it is not economically viable to produce the fabric in bulk. Minimum quantities are usually between 300 and 3000 metres. It is essential to ask the fabric supplier the minimum order quantity when viewing a fabric range as the buyer should know whether this is compatible with the anticipated garment order quantities. Occasionally a fabric supplier may be willing to sell fabric in less than the usual minimum quantity if the company is a very good customer, purchasing high quantities of other fabrics, or an extra charge per metre may be added to make the order financially viable. For printed fabrics the supplier may keep large quantities of base cloths in stock, onto which the print is applied. (The fabric supplier may not be the manufacturer of the base cloth, as it could be more cost-effective to import it.) A minimum order quantity applies to printed cloth as print screens and inks need to be specially developed for each design, and an order becomes worthwhile only if a substantial quantity is ordered. To estimate the amount of fabric required the average fabric usage per garment is calculated (see Chapter 7) and multiplied by the number of garments ordered. Fabric wastage must be included, as well as an allowance for garment rejects, to ensure that there is sufficient fabric to fulfil the total order.

Fabric development

At the beginning of a season buyers look for new ideas when viewing fabric ranges. This does not usually involve totally new concepts as customers are not generally receptive to drastic changes, particularly in the mass market. When sourcing new types of fabric, buyers may be looking for exactly the same cloth as the last season but with a different print, or perhaps the same type of fibre as the customer is used to but with a different weave from previous ranges. Developments in new fabrics for the high street tend therefore to be incremental, as the combination of a new mix of fibres, a new weave and a totally new colour palette would probably be too extreme and possibly too expensive for the store's customers. At ready-to-wear designer level, however, it is much more appropriate to introduce fabric innovations, as they serve a different type of customer who is actively seeking something different from the crowd and can afford the extra cost. Those fabrics which become popular at designer level later filter down to the high street, as do garment styles.

The cost of developing new fabrics is generally borne by fabric manufacturers as they continually have to introduce new ideas to keep customers interested and to compete with other suppliers. Of these new developments most will not become big sellers, but the few that go on to achieve large mass production orders of thousands of metres will compensate for this and offset relatively high development costs. Sometimes buyers find garments on a directional shopping trip, probably from a designer collection, in a fabric which they would like to include in a future range. It is rarely possible to find the original source out of the thousands of fabric manufacturers in the world so the buyer would probably show it to a company which specialises in similar types of fibres and construction to find out whether it was available. Sometimes this can mean sourcing the fabric by cutting up the original garment and sending swatches to several fabric manufacturers. (As this means effectively destroying a garment probably worth hundreds of pounds, swatches are often cut carefully from facings, hems and pockets, since buyers are reluctant to ruin expensive garments.) If the fabric is unavailable through the buyer's own sources a company may be asked to develop it specifically for the retailer. In this case the retailer usually needs to be able to buy very large quantities of garments to make the development costs sustainable. This depends also on the amount of development required varying from a slightly different finishing technique to the construction of a new type of weave which would cost substantially more. The fabric could be exclusive to the retailer who has initiated the development for the first season, but would probably be made available to other customers in future seasons to help offset some of the initial development costs.

Liaising with textile designers

Many buyers do not have the opportunity to deal directly with textile designers as they tend to liaise only with sales representatives. Liaising with textile designers, however, can give the buyer a greater say in the development of fabrics and can therefore be beneficial. Textile designers fall into two main categories, either designing the construction of the fabric (the weave or knit), or designing prints. Most textile designers work for fabric manufacturers either as full-time employees or on a freelance basis. Buyers rarely come into contact with such designers, sometimes because they are not based in the same country, but it is worthwhile for the buyer to request to meet fabric manufacturers' design teams to gain an understanding of the way in which they operate and to enhance the relationship with the supplier. Textile print designers can also be employed by clothing manufacturers and, to a lesser extent, by fashion retailers.

Some clothing manufacturers and retailers employ print designers to work closely with fashion designers, working mainly on CAD systems to recolour prints or to 'drape' them onto fashion drawings, in order to offer a complete design package of complementary garments and prints to retailers. Buyers may have regular meetings with in-house or garment manufacturers' print designers, to discuss the development of print ideas. Fashion buyers can also work directly with freelance print designers by commissioning print designs or by viewing the print designer's latest collection of artwork and purchasing a print, either at the retailer's head office, or at a trade fair such as *Indigo.*

Fabric imports and exports

Much of the garment production which takes place worldwide uses fabric which has been imported from other countries. The UK was formerly a major producer of textiles but its fabric production is now limited mainly to traditional woollen cloth, such as worsted and tweed, in the north of England and Scotland, and jersey fabrics are knitted in the east Midlands. There are also printers of a variety of knitted and woven cloths in the UK. It is not compulsory in the UK for garment manufacturers to state a garment's country of origin, and even if an item of clothing has a 'Made in UK' label, it is likely that the fabric is from overseas. Garment manufacturers, rather than retailers, are generally responsible for arranging the importation of fabrics. Many countries are renowned for specialising in certain fabric types and a fashion buyer who focuses on a particular product area, such as jerseywear, will probably work with several fabric and/or clothing manufacturers based in the same country, for example Turkey.

Fabric from the Far East and Europe

Certain countries specialise in particular fabrics and most of the fabrics sold within garments in the UK are imported from the Far East and Europe. China produces a wide range of cloths though in the past it was known mainly as the world's largest producer of silk in numerous weights and qualities. Japan is arguably the world's leading innovator in synthetic fabrics, including polyester and polyamide, and is renowned for good quality textiles. European countries are known more for fabric printing and jersey fabric production than for woven fabrics. France deals mainly with the printing of a variety of natural and synthetic cloths, particularly printed cotton for children's and ladies' wear. Germany, Italy and Portugal are also renowned for printed fabrics, especially on viscose basecloths. Greece and Turkey are mainly producers of jersey fabric, much of which is utilised within their local clothing industries. In the UK fabric production is limited mainly to traditional woollen cloth, for example worsted and tweed, in the north of England and Scotland. Jersey fabrics and hosiery are knitted in the east Midlands but this is a rapidly diminishing market. The UK has printers of both knitted and woven cloths.

Fabric prices

Fashion buyers need to ask suppliers several questions in relation to the price of fabric to discern its true value per metre. It is essential to know the width of the fabric, as it is obviously possible to manufacture more garments from wider fabric. Standard fabric widths are 112 cm and 150 cm, though other variations are sometimes available. It is essential for the buyer to note whether or not the quoted prices include delivery to the manufacturer. The lowest price is 'ex-mill' which means delivery is not included and it is literally just the price of producing the finished fabric. The buyer should either request the cost of delivery of the fabric or ask the clothing manufacturer to arrange for delivery, incorporating this cost within the final garment price. In order to do this the buyer needs to know in advance in which country the garments will be manufactured, possibly even before they have been designed. Prices can also be quoted 'FOB' (free on board) which includes the cost of delivery to a ship at the fabric manufacturer's nearest port. Ideally, the buyer should request a 'CIF' price (sometimes pronounced 'siff') meaning carriage, insurance and freight as this includes delivery to the garment manufacturer's premises and the goods will be insured whilst in transit. CIF prices can also be quoted for delivery to a port near to the manufacturer in which case the garment manufacturer will be responsible for arranging transport of the fabric to the factory.

The 'list price' per metre for fabric, which is initially quoted by the manufacturer, is the maximum price at which it will be sold and is unlikely to be the final price paid by most of the company's established customers. The buyer makes a note of the list price when initially viewing a fabric range, but a lower price can be negotiated if the buyer has a good relationship with the supplier or has a lot of buying power and works for a retailer which buys large quantities of garments. In this case the buyer has a maximum price in mind, for instance £4.10 for a fabric quoted at £4.20 per metre. If the full price is paid the buyer knows that the company's full margin cannot be achieved on the final garment. The buyer may initially offer £4 per metre, knowing that the fabric company's sales representative will probably meet halfway at £4.10 per metre. Negotiations are rarely this simple in practice but this gives an indication of the typical approach (see also Chapter 7). Sometimes a buyer can negotiate with factors other than price, perhaps by agreeing to pay the list price if the delivery lead time can be reduced from six to four weeks. This factor could be crucial to the profitability of a range by allowing the garments to be available to customers two weeks earlier.

Summary

Fashion buyers who develop own label ranges may participate in fabric sourcing. Fabrics are made from either natural or synthetic fibres (or a mixture of both) and can be of a knitted or woven construction. Fabrics can be treated by dyeing, printing or finishing techniques or embellished after production. Buyers and designers source fabrics by contacting representatives of suppliers and viewing fabric collections, which are updated each season. Many buyers attend the *Première Vision* fabric fair to identify trends and to source fabrics.

Further reading

Anstey, H. and Weston, T. (1997) *The Anstey Weston Guide to Textile Terms.* Weston Publishing, London.

Braddock, S. and O'Mahony, M. (2005) *Techno Textiles: Revolutionary Fabrics for Fashion and Design No. 2.* Thames & Hudson, London.

Gale, C. and Kaur, J. (2002) *The Textile Book.* Berg, London.

Goworek, H. (2006) *Careers in Fashion and Textiles.* Blackwell Publishing, Oxford.

Wells, K. (1997) *Fabric Dyeing and Printing.* Conran Octopus, London.

Chapter 7

Garment Sourcing

Selecting manufacturers to supply merchandise is a significant responsibility for all fashion buyers. In order to make a suitable decision about which manufacturer to select to produce a certain style the buyer needs to assess many factors including:

- reliability and previous performance
- price
- production quality
- speed of production and delivery
- quality of service and reputation, e.g. design and sampling
- ethical issues
- supplier audits for these factors in new and existing factories.

It is extremely useful for fashion buyers to have an understanding of the way in which clothing suppliers operate, to be aware of whether their demands are realistic, for example in terms of sampling timescale and the complexity of garment styling. Spending time within a factory environment is beneficial for buyers, to enable them to comprehend more easily the realities of garment production and to build positive partnerships with suppliers.

Methods of garment sourcing

Methods of garment sourcing vary depending on the company's buying policy. Some stores source garments by more than one method, for example Whistles develop their own garment range as well as offering items from own-label designers.

Selecting garments from manufacturers' existing ranges

This is particularly appropriate for retailers who wish to offer a wide variety of merchandise to several different types of customer, such as department stores. It is also appropriate for small independent stores who cannot buy merchandise in sufficient volume to make the development of their own ranges viable.

Such ranges usually carry the label of the manufacturer or brand rather than the retailer. Garments can be selected from the manufacturers by visiting a showroom or trade fair, or a sales representative can visit the buyer to present the range. This is usually the most straightforward method of buying fashion merchandise as it involves selecting finalised garments rather than being involved in design and product development decisions.

Product development between buyers and garment manufacturers

This involves the buyer viewing ranges from manufacturers either as garment samples or sketches, and making relevant amendments like changing colours and fabrics, proportions, fit or trims. This method is popular with buyers for many mass market retailers, making the development of the range a joint effort between the buyer and the manufacturer's design department. One advantage of this method is that many manufacturers have valuable sales information about which styles, fabrics and colours are selling well to some of their other retail customers. Sales figures are of course confidential, but the garment manufacturer is able to advise the buyer on which styles could sell well in future seasons. The buyer may also ask the manufacturer's design department to develop ideas based on sketches, magazine cuttings or garments from a directional shopping trip. Product development and production within a clothing factory obviously run concurrently with the retailer's critical path. The processes involved from the manufacturer's perspective are detailed in Figure 7.1 and should be compared to the buying cycle (Figure 3.1) and critical path of the retailer. There can be variations to the product development processes listed here depending on the way in which the retailer and manufacturer involved operate. Certain stages may be removed to save time and/or money, e.g. for fast fashion or low-price styles, e.g. buyers may select products from drawings rather than samples, particularly if they are high-resolution CAD images, speeding up the selection process.

Selecting garments to retailers' own specifications

This method gives the retailer tight control over the coordination of a range and is used by those retailers who are considered to be design-led with a strong coordinated image for their merchandise. Such retailers usually have in-house design teams and provide garment specification sheets (often abbreviated to 'spec.' sheets), containing detailed written and visual information on styling, design details, fabric and trims, to their suppliers. Retailers who work in this way need to be able to buy relatively large volumes of garments to make the overheads of employing a design team and developing the product worthwhile. The minimum order quantity required to buy merchandise by this method is usually at least 500 pieces per style and many manufacturers, particularly overseas suppliers, require orders of at least 2000 pieces.

Certain retailers provide the manufacturer with a fully detailed spec. sheet including a working drawing (a precise technical drawing of a garment), fabric

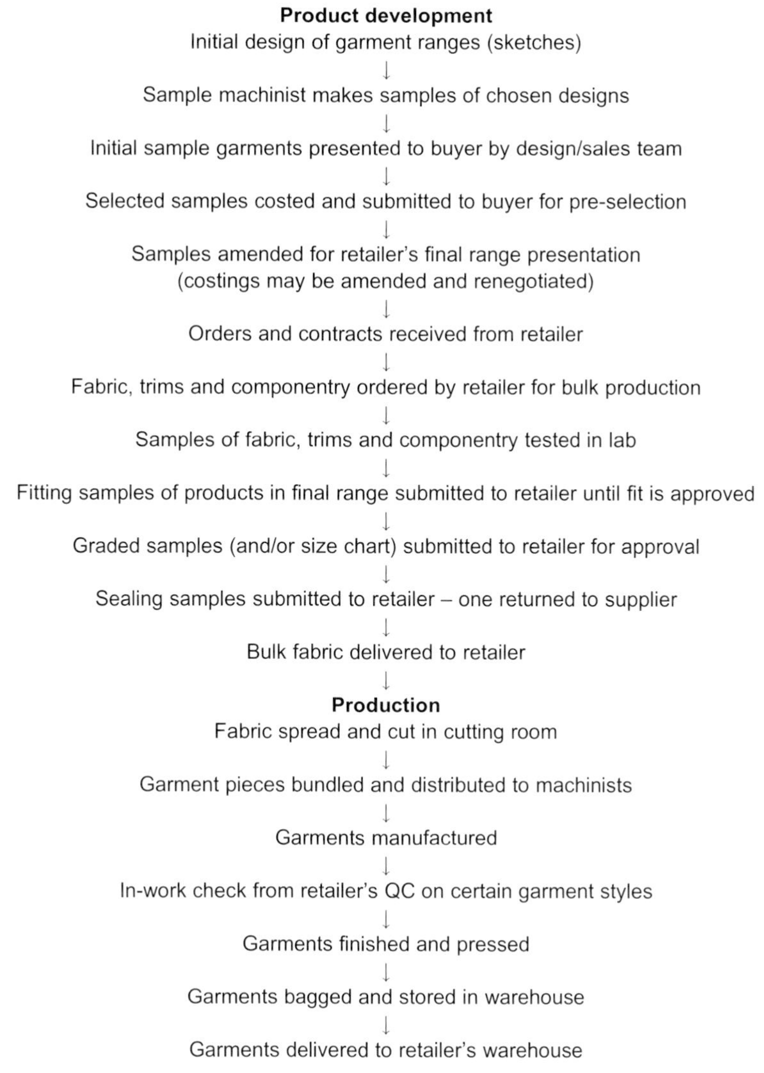

Product development
Initial design of garment ranges (sketches)
↓
Sample machinist makes samples of chosen designs
↓
Initial sample garments presented to buyer by design/sales team
↓
Selected samples costed and submitted to buyer for pre-selection
↓
Samples amended for retailer's final range presentation
(costings may be amended and renegotiated)
↓
Orders and contracts received from retailer
↓
Fabric, trims and componentry ordered by retailer for bulk production
↓
Samples of fabric, trims and componentry tested in lab
↓
Fitting samples of products in final range submitted to retailer until fit is approved
↓
Graded samples (and/or size chart) submitted to retailer for approval
↓
Sealing samples submitted to retailer – one returned to supplier
↓
Bulk fabric delivered to retailer
↓
Production
Fabric spread and cut in cutting room
↓
Garment pieces bundled and distributed to machinists
↓
Garments manufactured
↓
In-work check from retailer's QC on certain garment styles
↓
Garments finished and pressed
↓
Garments bagged and stored in warehouse
↓
Garments delivered to retailer's warehouse

Figure 7.1 The product development and production process in a clothing factory.

information and trim details. The manufacturer then makes the garment patterns and a sample garment. A length of fabric to make the sample garment is sometimes provided by the retailer, having been selected from a fabric manufacturer's range. Some retailers take this method of buying a stage further by having the patterns made in-house and passing them to the garment supplier to make a first sample. Manufacturers who operate in this way, focusing solely on garment production without an in-house design team, are known as 'cut, make and trim' (CMT) garment suppliers. (This is similar to the way in which ready-to-wear fashion designers operate, though designer labels tend to sell in much smaller quantities and therefore work with small specialist manufacturers.) A limited number of fashion retailers have an in-house sample room where some of their initial design concept garments can be produced to present to suppliers.

Liaising with garment suppliers

Buyers may deal directly with representatives from any of the following, when buying merchandise, at home or overseas:

- garment manufacturers
- the retailer's overseas sourcing office
- agents
- indirect importers
- wholesalers.

The buyer usually liaises with a representative from the sales department of the manufacturer and may also be in direct contact with designers or garment technologists from the company, who may be based in the UK or overseas. The relationship between buyer and supplier is crucial to the success of a retailer and should ideally be mutually supportive. Effective buyers maintain communication with their suppliers by informing them promptly of any updates regarding their products.

As an extremely high level of clothing sold in the UK is imported, garment sourcing is one of the main opportunities for travel by the buyer. Time must be planned very carefully on business trips as companies invest a large amount of money in travel and every hour must be used to the maximum. Evenings and weekends are likely to be spent socialising with business associates or working. There is a huge difference between holidays and sourcing trips. Occasionally buyers may be fortunate enough to take some of their holiday entitlement immediately after a business trip at a nearby location. However this is seldom the case as the buyer will have plenty of work to catch up on at Head Office. The timing of the trip is important – it needs to be early enough to put garments into work with enough time to develop and finalise the range afterwards.

The demise of the UK clothing industry

Garment manufacturing diminished in the UK during the 1980s and 1990s, exemplified by Marks and Spencer's severance in 1999 of a long-standing contract with the UK manufacturer, William Baird, resulting in the purchase of more goods in other countries. By 1998, 73.6% of clothing sold in the UK was manufactured overseas (Key Note, 2000) and by 2005 this figure had risen to 95% (Key Note, 2006a). Coats Viyella (CV) ceased producing merchandise for Marks and Spencer in 2000, resulting in the closure of several UK factories and many job losses, despite their having been the retailer's largest supplier. (Several parts of the CV group were renamed Quantum in a management buyout and continue to supply clothing to UK retailers, most of which is now imported.)

Between 1998 and 2004, the number of employees working for UK clothing manufacturers fell by a staggering 75% (Key Note, 2006b). Much of this contraction is the result of UK manufacturers relocating their production to lower-cost countries such as the People's Republic of China and India. Such a profound loss of manufacturing has significantly reduced the UK clothing industry's former status as the fifth largest employer in the UK. However, a limited number of clothing factories remain in the UK distributed throughout the country but concentrated mainly around London, the east Midlands and Manchester. The companies which are successful in this country compete more on service than price, offering a fast turnaround of products, a design service and/or good quality. An increasing number of companies offer overseas production, using a UK-based design team. This is confirmed by the following comments from Key Note's (2006a) report on the UK Clothing and Footwear Industry:

> The successful UK companies concentrate on specialist or premium products . . . Manufacturing is taking a backseat and designers – often working separately from manufacturers – marketers and distributors are coming to the fore . . . The rise of cheap imports has been near-fatal for much of UK manufacturing, where employment has slumped from nearly half a million in the 1980's to less than 140,000 by 2005.

Buying fashion merchandise overseas

Price is an obvious advantage in buying fashion merchandise overseas, as evidenced by the relatively low cost (and standard) of living in the countries which are the major producers of UK clothing imports:

- The Far East
- India
- Bangladesh
- Turkey
- Eastern Europe (Retail Intelligence, 2005).

There are also manufacturing techniques and skills which are available only in certain countries, e.g. embroidered cotton products from India, and the prestige of buying from fashion-orientated countries such as Italy. Buying fashion merchandise overseas does have a number of disadvantages, however:

- long-distance delivery costs
- import charges, such as duties and quotas (in some cases)
- longer delivery time
- quality standards can be more difficult to monitor
- time and expense incurred by buyer in travelling to overseas markets and communicating
- buying in a different currency.

Other potential problems when buying products from overseas include:

- language barriers
- time difference
- unethical practices (e.g. child labour)
- political unrest and war
- strikes (e.g. lorry drivers)
- currency fluctuations
- variable weather conditions (e.g. flooding).

Most of the disadvantages in buying merchandise abroad can be overcome, and are usually outweighed by the price advantage or the distinctive nature of the product. Computers have assisted the process of overseas sourcing through easier access to information on companies via internet searches. www.apparelsearch.com and www.fibre2fashion.com are examples of websites offering access to various global garment manufacturers. Email has overtaken phone and letters as the prime method of international communication. When buyers are away assistants are usually left to oversee ranges in their absence, which can give them an opportunity to gain valuable experience in carrying out the buyer's role on a short-term basis. During buying trips overseas buyers are usually in regular contact with head office, but assistant buyers may find that situations arise which require a rapid response, resulting in the need for decisions to be taken during a buyer's absence.

Under the terms of the Multi Fibre Agreement (MFA) which was implemented in 1974, a limited amount of goods, referred to as quota, was permitted to be exported from China to the UK. Individual Chinese manufacturers were allowed an amount of quota, that is to export a certain quantity of garments, and a trade developed where quota was sold on the open market. The cost of quota varied from one season to another depending on demand for it and according to the product category of the merchandise. After the cessation of the MFA in January 2005 Chinese clothing exports to the UK increased overwhelmingly, owing to the withdrawal of quota. This was detrimental to garment manufacturers in other countries as buyers had been tempted to increase business with China, because of its more competitive prices and the removal of volume restrictions on merchandise imported from there. The EU's response was to bring imports from China to a standstill, leaving an estimated 80 million garments stranded in suppliers or in customs in a political situation the press dubbed 'bra wars'. This was problematic for buyers awaiting delivery of merchandise into stores, but more significantly it was extremely disruptive to the Chinese factories and their employees. A temporary solution was sought through a 'Memorandum of Understanding' between the EU and China in June 2005, which allowed exporting to recommence with the reimposition of quotas. It could be argued that the situation still requires a permanent resolution.

The advantages and disadvantages of buying fashion merchandise from the European market are generally the opposite of those for buying from other continents. In theory, delivery time should be reduced when purchasing goods closer to home and it should be easier to monitor quality standards. However, if goods are delivered by air freight from the Far East this can take just a few days longer than goods being transported by road in the same continent. Some of the potential problems mentioned above can also apply to buying products in Europe, for instance unethical practices, strikes and adverse weather conditions can affect almost any country. There is an increasing trend for retailers to replace their European manufacturing sources with garment imports from north African countries such as Tunisia, Morocco and Egypt.

It is possible for sample garments to be received by UK buyers relatively quickly from overseas manufacturers, despite the distance. International courier services which can deliver in as short a time as two days make overseas manufacturers very competitive in terms of speed of sample development. Products are invariably more expensive to manufacture in Western than in Eastern countries, mainly owing to higher labour costs. It could be considered unethical to purchase products from countries where machinists are paid low wages, yet by deciding to buy products elsewhere the buyer could deprive these workers of their only source of income. The wages of the machinists should also be considered in relation to their cost of living which is much lower in most Eastern countries than in the Western hemisphere, but buyers should make decisions about garment sourcing in light of the moral and ethical issues involved.

Ethical sourcing issues

Ethical trading has become a key issue for fashion retailers in recent years, spurred on by increasing consumer demand for products made in conditions which respect workers' rights. As garment production moves increasingly offshore, consumers are taking an interest in the source of the products they purchase. The major American fashion companies Nike, Gap and Wal-mart have gained negative publicity in the press during the past decade amid accusations that some of their merchandise is produced in offshore sweatshops, culminating in a public admission and apology for this practice from Nike. Robert Greenwald's 2005 film *Wal-mart – the High Cost of Low Price* is an exposé of the American supermarket giant's dealings with staff and suppliers, offering viewers a revealing insight into its practices, further heightening the public's awareness of debatable business ethics.

The issue of ethical sourcing is currently so significant that the Association of Suppliers to the British Clothing Industry (ASBCI) based their 2006 conference on the subject. It was reported there that current monthly wages in clothing manufacture average $125 in China, $65 in India and $30 in Bangladesh, revealing some of the vast differences in labour rates between developing countries. It was also stated at the ASBCI conference that £43m had been spent by consumers on ethical clothing in the UK in 2005.

Ecological aspects of ethical trading in fashion focus mostly on health and safety, with the use of chemicals in textile production, particularly pesticides and dyestuffs, high on the agenda. People Tree (see case study in this chapter) and Gossypium are amongst the fashion businesses taking ecology seriously by utilising 'green' textiles in their products, such as organic cotton, which is grown without the use of health-endangering pesticides. Snowboard and the BMX clothing brand Howies use an alternative environmentally friendly approach by selling garments manufactured from recycled cotton fabric.

The Fairtrade Foundation produce a consumer label which they describe as 'an independent guarantee that disadvantaged producers in the developing world are getting a better deal' (www.fairtrade.co.uk, 2006). Products bearing this label must meet international standards and be certified by Fairtrade Labelling Organizations International (FLO). Fairtrade producers are paid a minimum price for their goods plus a premium that contributes towards development projects in the region. After committing to selling only Fairtrade coffee and tea in its cafes, Marks and Spencer introduced T-shirts and socks made from Fairtrade cotton in March 2006. Later in the same year, they launched men's and women's Fairtrade cotton jeans, T-shirts and underwear, followed by a range of Fairtrade and organic cotton babywear (www2.marksandspencer.com, 2006).

In 2005 Bono, Ali Hewson and the designer Rogan Gregory launched the fashion brand 'Edun' describing it as a 'socially conscious clothing company'. Though it is not certified by the Fairtrade Foundation, Edun has a compatible aim: to offer trade, rather than aid, to developing countries such as Africa and India, to develop sustainable employment. The concept behind it has been described as 'a plan that starts with what the factory makes and then takes that to the world, rather than planning to find the cheapest factory in the world and move on when another factory charges less' (Sullivan, 2005: 257).

The designer Katharine Hamnett is renowned for incorporating her political stance into her collections and has undoubtedly helped the cause for ethical sourcing by becoming a vociferous campaigner on the topic. She is introducing the 'Katharine E Hamnett' label in 2007, incorporating organic cotton into menswear and womenswear which is ethically manufactured by carefully selected suppliers, many of whom she has visited in person to guarantee their credentials. A key aspect of this range is that it is undistinguishable in terms of fashionability from her usual collections.

The Clean Clothes Campaign (CCC) is an international pressure group (formed from coalitions between non-governmental organisations (NGO) and trade unions in nine European countries in collaboration with organisations in non-European garment-producing countries) which strives to improve working conditions in the global garment industry (www.cleanclothes.org, 2006). Labour Behind the Label, the UK arm of CCC, aims to raise consumer awareness in addition to lobbying companies and government about these issues (www.labourbehindthelabel.org, 2006).

It is now becoming standard practice for UK retailers to develop corporate and social responsibility (CSR) policies pertaining to their methods of garment sourcing and partnerships with suppliers. Marks and Spencer have taken this a step further with their recent 'Look Behind The Label' campaign, which encourages people to consider the manufacturers behind their products, being promoted directly to customers. Various major retailers have also addressed the issue by appointing managers within their quality control teams with direct responsibility for ethical sourcing.

The Ethical Trading Initiative (ETI) is a collaboration between companies, NGOs and trade unions set up in 1998. The ETI's website states that its aims are: 'to promote and improve the implementation of corporate codes of practice which cover supply chain working conditions. Our ultimate goal is to ensure that the working conditions of workers producing for the UK market meet or exceed international labour standards' (www.ethicaltrade.org, 2006). The ETI's membership inevitably includes Marks and Spencer as well as Asda, New Look, Tesco and Primark in addition to international retailers such as Zara and Gap.

Overseas sourcing offices

A retailer's overseas sourcing office is usually staffed mostly by merchandisers, whose role varies substantially from that of a head office-based merchandiser. In an overseas sourcing office merchandisers represent the retailer whilst understanding the market of the country in which they are based, both in terms of language and culture. This type of merchandiser is often a native of the country where the office is located, but many companies also employ expatriates in key roles within an overseas sourcing office. Merchandisers from the overseas sourcing office usually liaise with buyers, merchandisers and QCs from the retailer's head office on a daily basis. The advantage to buyers is that they can communicate via just one person in that country rather than with several representatives from manufacturers. Merchandisers from the overseas office sometimes visit buyers at the company's UK head office to be briefed on the direction of the next season's range, thereby allowing them to consult manufacturers and prepare effectively before the buyer travels to the country on a buying trip.

Only relatively large retailers can usually afford to run overseas sourcing offices, as the overheads are reasonably high and can only be met by companies which buy garments in large quantities. Many large store groups have their own offices in the capitals of the world's main clothing manufacturers, such as Delhi and Hong Kong. Independent garment sourcing offices exist in numerous countries, offering their services to various retail clients who do not have their own offices in those locations. In the USA there are many independent buying offices providing the facility to source products, aimed primarily at American retailers (Clodfelter, 2003).

During visits overseas buyers may have meetings with the manufacturers either at the retailer's office base or at the manufacturer's showroom (which may be based within the factory premises). The retailer's overseas merchandiser is usually present at these meetings to take notes, help with liaison (particularly language problems) and to follow up on behalf of the buyer after the meeting. Figure 7.2 shows a UK buyer visiting a manufacturer's showroom

Figure 7.2 Buying meeting with a supplier in India.

in India, accompanied by a merchandiser from the overseas sourcing office. Buyers contact overseas manufacturers regularly, either directly or through the overseas merchandise office. This is to follow up on the progress of issues such as approvals of lab dyes, strike-offs, fitting samples and fabric tests, primarily by email, but also by fax and phone.

Agents and indirect importers

Buyers can also work with agents, based either in the UK or abroad. The agents are paid by the suppliers with whom they work on a salary and/or commission basis. The advantage of working in this way is that the retailer does not need to invest in setting up an office abroad. However, agents sell products from a limited number of companies, which may give the buyer less scope for initiating relationships with new suppliers. An agent effectively undertakes a sales role for the manufacturers, and is usually paid on a commission-only basis, increasing the incentive for selling a high quantity of merchandise to the buyer. Indirect importers work in a similar way to agents. They are based in the UK, developing products to sell to retailers and then organising the manufacture of the garments overseas, probably working with more than one factory. The manufacturer pays the indirect importer a percentage of the income which has been generated by this method. The indirect importer is therefore taking on much of the garment sourcing role from the buyer, and products sold in this way cost slightly more than if the buyer were working directly with factories abroad, to cover the indirect importer's costs.

Exchange rates

At the start of a buying season the buyer is briefed on the season's exchange rates, usually by the imports or merchandise department. As exchange rates fluctuate it is essential that buyers refer to the latest rate or their calculations (and therefore profit margins) will be incorrect. Foreign currency is purchased in advance by retailers so the rate a buyer uses is based on the rate at the time of purchase of the currency and therefore does not change daily.

Wholesalers

Some buyers purchase products from wholesalers, who are effectively 'middlemen'. The wholesaler buys quantities of garments from manufacturers which are then kept in stock, to be sold on to retailers. The wholesaler's premises take the form of a warehouse filled with bulk quantities of garments which are available for immediate delivery to retailers. Wholesalers may also have a showroom with samples of current styles to show to buyers and, possibly, samples of garments to be produced in the future. Buying from a wholesaler is a method used mainly by small-scale retailers, particularly fashion stores with one outlet, or market traders, because it is possible to buy small quantities of garments from stock. Some wholesalers are willing to sell as few as ten pieces of a garment, though the wholesaler may charge a little extra for such a small order. The garments cost more from a wholesaler than if the retailer ordered them directly from the manufacturer but most small-scale retailers would be unlikely to buy big enough quantities to order directly from a factory. The advantage of buying from a wholesaler is that the garments are available from stock rather than having to order months in advance, and if the retailer sells out of a style it may be possible to order more garments at short notice. Ready-to-wear designers and many branded fashion labels effectively operate wholesale operations by ordering quantities of styles that they have designed in-house from manufacturers, and subsequently selling it to retailers.

Minimum and initial orders

When a buyer selects a garment style, the garment quantity is often decided after discussion with the merchandiser. If the garment is being produced exclusively for a retailer this should be at least the minimum production quantity permitted by the manufacturer. For an own label retailer it could possibly be as few as 500 but is more often in excess of 1000 pieces per style. If the buyer is selecting a garment from an existing range, usually with a different label from that of the retailer, it is feasible for the minimum quantity to be as low as ten garments. This is because the manufacturer is producing many more of the same garment, to be sold to several different stores. Manufacturers have minimum order quantities because it is not usually financially viable to produce small quantities, as the machinists do not have the opportunity to attain an economical speed of manufacture with a relatively small run. Also overheads, such as the costs of pattern cutting and grading, which are usually borne by the manufacturer, are relatively high if spread over a small number of garments. At designer level, the ready-to-wear sector of the fashion market, design development and pattern cutting take place at the designer's studio and manufacturers can make very small quantities – as little as 20 pieces – for which they charge a premium price. At this level of the market manufacture usually takes place in small factories with highly skilled machinists who may need to be more versatile in their sewing skills than in a mass production clothing factory.

Placing repeat orders with suppliers

The buyer must make an informed decision about how many garments to order initially, perhaps choosing to be cautious by ordering the minimum amount possible. However if the product sells well and the initial estimate was overcautious the retailer may be in danger of being out of stock of a successful line, consequently losing orders and therefore missing out on potential profits. If an initial order of a garment style sells well the buyer or merchandiser may consider purchasing a repeat order which will usually be purchased from the original garment manufacturer, though this can vary. If the initial order was bought from China, for example, the delivery time for a repeat could be too long for the product to arrive in store for the current season. In this case the buyer may decide to order the product from the original supplier but have it delivered by air rather than sea, thereby speeding up the delivery schedule by weeks. Although air freight is expensive, the garment obviously appeals to the retailers' customers, and it is likely to continue to sell well. The buyer may therefore be prepared to take a lower profit margin, though this may require approval from either the senior buyer or buying manager.

If the design idea for a bestselling style manufactured in the Far East belongs to the retailer, the buyer may place a repeat order in a closer location such as Turkey or Egypt, and although the production costs are likely to be more expensive, delivery time should – in theory – be quicker. However the manufacturer may need to add time to the production schedule to develop patterns and samples as the original supplier is unlikely to be willing to send copies of patterns to a competitor. In this example the buyer needs to draw on experience, and possibly advice from colleagues, as to which country to choose for a repeat order. The main method of assessing the need for repeat orders is to calculate the number of weeks of 'cover' available for a garment, that is, how many more weeks the garment is likely to stay in stock. Some retailers see ten weeks cover as being ideal; so from an initial order of 3000 garments, 300 pieces will have sold in the first week. This is a simplistic example, as sales usually tend to be boosted when the product first arrives in store, trailing off later in the season. However this is not always the case as some products may be delivered prior to a trend taking hold, or magazine coverage of a garment may generate high mid-season sales figures. The timing for repeat orders is crucial and if the manufacturer does not deliver by a specified time the product may be literally past its sell-by date. Racks of garments in the January sales may not be caused solely by the buyer selecting the wrong type of product for the customer, but may also be due to repeat orders arriving too late for the season.

Departments within a garment supplier

The departmental structure of a garment factory varies from one company to another and is often dependent on the size of the organisation, large-scale manufacturers usually having more departments than smaller companies. Companies with fewer than 100 employees require versatile individuals who may be expected to take on dual roles, for instance production/quality control manager, or designer/pattern cutter. A clothing manufacturer is typically divided into the following departments:

- design
- sales and marketing
- costings
- purchasing
- QC
- cutting room
- production
- finishing
- warehouse.

In smaller factories some of these departments may be merged. Some companies have a centralized design and sales office, which develops products for one or more factories in other locations. All of the manufacturer's departments should interact in order to complete orders successfully. It is a sign of a positive working environment when the supplier's design and sales staff liaise with QC and production during the design and sampling process.

Design department

A supplier may have one designer or a design team headed by a manager. The design department is usually located in a separate room (or sometimes even a separate country) from production, with storage facilities for fabric samples, patterns and reference material. Designers may be responsible for cutting patterns for their designs, or there may be specialist pattern cutters and graders. Each designer focuses on one or more retailers. The first sample of a design is usually made to the designer's specifications by a sample machinist, usually based in the factory where the product will be manufactured, who completes all of the sewing operations within the garment. Designers need to be aware of production constraints such as the type of sewing machines available in the factory in order to design garments which are suitable for bulk production, and sample machinists can be very helpful in this respect at the design stage.

Designers are involved throughout the product development stage of a garment and may be consulted during production, for example to check if the bulk fabric delivery and trims are of the correct type.

Sales and marketing

Smaller manufacturers may have one sales representative whereas a large-scale clothing supplier may have a sales and marketing department headed by a director. The sales team are responsible for liaising with retailers to sell the company's products and for negotiating prices. Sales representatives need to know the potential volume of production available in the factory so that they can assess how many garments they need to sell to keep the machinists in work. Meetings with retailers are usually attended jointly by a sales representative and designer, with the sales representative concentrating on prices and order quantities while the designer discusses styling and fabrics. Sales representatives are involved mainly during the product development phase of garments but also take an active interest in production, as they are responsible for liaising with merchandisers to ensure that the agreed deadline and delivery dates will be met.

Costings

The supplier may have a costing team, or costing may be incorporated into a sales or production role. Garment suppliers submit costings to retailers by estimating accurately the price of manufacturing the garment plus all of the materials and trims, and a profit margin to make the sale financially viable. Buyers frequently request cost prices within a short space of time but for the price to be accurate a garment sample should be made first and analysed, so it is more difficult for a realistic cost price to be given from a garment sketch. However an experienced sales representative or designer may be able to estimate the cost price from a sketch instinctively, allowing them to give an estimated figure to the buyer.

Stages in producing a costing

(1) The design department documents relevant information such as the type of buttons and material for a style, to be sent to the factory. The designer has a great deal of influence on the costing through the selection of fabric, trims and design details within the garment.

(2) Once the sample garment has been made the sample machinist may be asked to list every separate process involved, passing this on to a garment technician, who estimates how long a garment will take, on average, to complete in bulk production. Because every machinist works at varying speeds the time can only ever be estimated, based on numerous time studies compiled from observing machinists on previous production runs. The average time which a machinist is expected to take to sew a garment can be estimated in what are known as 'standard minutes'.

(3) The pattern-cutter or lay-planner estimates the average quantity of fabric required per garment. (It is useful for accuracy at this stage to know the size range for the style, as larger sizes will obviously use more fabric.)

(4) The price of the fabric per metre and all trims and components for the garment need to be estimated, possibly by the supplier's merchandiser or purchasing department (see below).

(5) The estimated standard minutes can be communicated to the person responsible for the costing, where they are combined with the information about the quantities and prices of materials and components, and a computer program may be used to calculate a suggested price.

(6) The sales representative can then analyse the costing sheet and presents an initial price to the buyer. This price is based largely on the estimated production and material costs but is also influenced by how much the customer is expected to pay. The salesperson negotiates with the buyer until a price is finalised which is agreeable to both parties. The final selling price from the manufacturer to the retailer is referred to as the cost price.

Purchasing

The person responsible for purchasing the fabric and components necessary to make garments is often referred to as a buyer, yet the role differs substantially from the job of the fashion buyer employed by a retailer. Large manufacturers may have a department devoted to this task, based either in the UK or overseas, and in others it may form part of the sales, merchandising or production role. A buyer working for a manufacturer is essentially an administrator who completes the necessary paperwork to order specified fabrics and trims, and may become involved in negotiating the most competitive prices for these products from the suppliers.

Quality control

Factories usually employ more than one QC, depending on the size of the company, responsible for checking the standard of merchandise being produced. In a large company there may be a QC manager responsible for coordinating the QC team and setting standards of garment make-up. The QC manager liaises with retailers' QC teams when they visit factories for in-work checks, or may be responsible for self-certifying inspections to retailers' quality standards. Some manufacturers employ garment technologists in a similar role.

Cutting room

Although most garment factories have their own cutting rooms in which fabric is laid out and cut for bulk orders, some companies specialise only in cutting garments, used either by small factories which concentrate purely on making garments, or by larger factories which need extra cutting capacity at busy periods. When the grades for a garment have been approved the patterns are arranged in what is known as a 'lay plan' to achieve the minimum of fabric wastage by a 'marker maker' (who may be based in the cutting room) either manually or by computer. For bulk production fabric is laid out in several piles by specialist spreading machines before cutting, and the lay plan is placed on top. Most factories use a straightknife, powered by an electric motor, which a cutter uses to cut through many layers of fabric at once guided by the lay plan. Laser cutting, water jet cutting and ultrasonic cutting are new developments which may eventually supersede the straightknife. Cut work is labelled and bundled and sent for garment production.

Garment production

A production manager is responsible for planning and implementing garment production. Factories are usually organised in production lines where machinists are seated in rows and work is delivered to them in bundles by supervisors (see Figure 7.3). The basic types of sewing machine used in the industry are lockstitchers and overlockers. The lockstitch machine has a basic stitch similar to that of a domestic machine, and is used for joining seams, topstitching, and many other garment manufacturing techniques. An overlocker finishes the raw edges of seams and hems to avoid fraying.

There are also numerous types of specialist sewing machine including seamcover machines and flatseamers which are suitable for making garments in stretch fabrics. The type of sewing machines used by a factory can vary according to the type of garments produced. Garment factories tend to specialise in either woven or knitted fabrics, and it is essential that the buyer is aware of a manufacturer's specialisation in fabric and garment type when placing a style in production. Make-up of garments is split into separate operations so

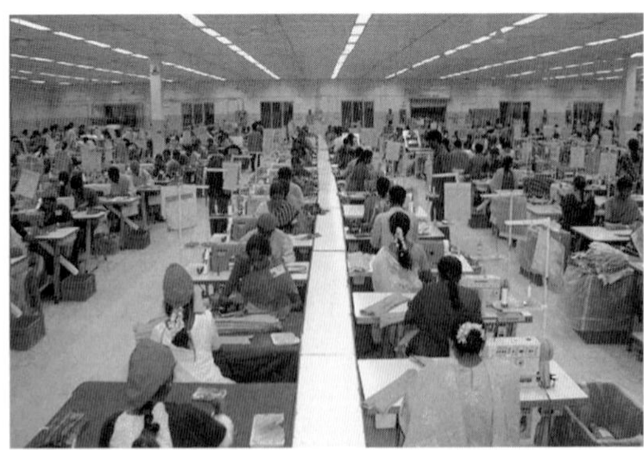

Figure 7.3 P.S. Apparel clothing factory, Tamilnadu, India. Courtesy of RK Industries, Chennai, India.

that some machinists specialise in making up certain elements of a garment, such as collars, or certain types of machining such as overlocking the seams together. Supervisors are experienced machinists responsible for organising a production line. A more traditional method of factory organisation is for an individual machinist or a small team, to 'make through' garments from start to finish, though this is now relatively rare. A team of pressers iron the finished garments and some garments may be sent through a steam tunnel. Completed garments are checked during and after production by QCs, and faulty garments are returned to the machinists who produced them, to be corrected. Defective garments which cannot be corrected, or which have fabric faults, are referred to as seconds and are not submitted to the retailer.

Warehousing and delivery

Finished garments are bagged in transparent plastic garment covers to keep them clean, then stored in the factory's warehouse either in boxes or on hangers. A final garment inspection by the factory's or retailer's QCs may take place in the warehouse. The garments are then delivered to the retailer's warehouse where there may be a final QC inspection before distribution of the products to stores.

Summary

Buyers make decisions on garment sourcing based mainly on the price, quality and service of the manufacturer. High street retailers usually develop garment ideas in conjunction with manufacturers, liaising mostly with designers and sales representatives from their suppliers. The vast majority of clothing sold in the UK is imported, though many garment suppliers have a UK-based design and sales team using overseas production. The product development and production processes run simultaneously with the retailer's buying cycle. Consumer awareness of ethical sourcing issues is increasing and retailers are responding by developing corporate and social responsibility policies and practice in their dealings with suppliers.

References and further reading

Clodfelter, R. (2003) *Retail Buying: from Basics to Fashion*. Fairchild, New York.
Key Note (2000) *Clothing Manufacturing May 2000*. Key Note, London.
Key Note (2006a) *Clothing and Footwear Industry Market Review March 2006*. Key Note, London.
Key Note (2006b) *Clothing Manufacturing May 2006*. Key Note, London.
Retail Intelligence (2005) *Clothing Retailing July 2005*. Mintel, London.
Rivoli, P. (2005) *The Travels of a T-shirt in the Global Economy*. Wiley, Hoboken, NJ.
Sullivan, R. (2005) Stream of Conscience. *Vogue* (USA), March 2005: 524–31.

Websites

www.asbci.co.uk
www.cleanclothes.org
www.ethicaltrade.org
www.fairtrade.co.uk
www.ifat.org
www.labourbehindthelabel.org
www2.marksandspencer.com/thecompany/trustyour_mands/fairtrade.shtml
www.peopletree.co.uk
www.un.org/millenniumgoals/

CASE STUDY IN ETHICAL GARMENT SOURCING

People Tree

Safia Minney founded People Tree in the UK in 2001 (see Figure 7.4), having launched its predecessor the Fair Trade Company and Global Village in 1991 in Japan. Prior to this she worked in PR, marketing and communications in the publishing industry, including four years at *Creative Review* magazine, and ran her own communications consultancy for four years. People Tree sell Fair Trade and ecological womenswear, menswear and childrenswear via their website, catalogue and various fashion retailers, including Selfridges. The company describes Fair Trade as 'a partnership between producers and traders, which aims at sustainable development for excluded and disadvantaged people in developing countries'.

The aims of the company

When asked to describe People Tree's main aims Safia says:

> We're very development-based and led. We felt that people wanted to buy Fair Trade handicrafts and food and clothing. In terms of the British context a lot of people will buy Fair Trade foods but we haven't really had that offer yet in Fair Trade fashion. People want to know that products are made with respect for the people and for the environment. If there's some way of promoting sustainable development and poverty alleviation through making a product people would want to support Fair Trade fashion. They also want to support companies that are campaigning to clean up the fashion industry.
>
> We don't start with profits and what delivers the biggest margins to the company. We start with the producers and what traditional skills they have. How can we create work and promote livelihoods in very rural areas? What we're trying to do is to use trade to help people escape from poverty. For example

Figure 7.4 People Tree founder Safia Minney. Courtesy of People Tree.

Cont.

Case study *Continued.*

we use fabrics that are hand-woven because we can employ 15 people to do this, as opposed to only one if it was made on a power loom. We choose to use handwoven rather than mass-produced fabric so that we can employ large numbers of people and spread the benefits of trade more widely. In a rural area where unemployment is 50% or more you have an ability to help people to feed themselves, earn a good income, educate their children and develop their communities, giving the people a chance to use Fair Trade to escape from poverty and build sustainable ways to produce products and trading.

People Tree's Fair Trade policies are:

- to pay producers fair prices
- to make advance payments when needed
- to promote traditional skills
- to promote rural development
- to operate with transparency.

The company's eco policies are:

- to promote natural and organic cotton farming
- to avoid using damaging chemicals
- to use natural, recycled and biodegradable substances where possible
- to recycle where possible
- to protect water supplies and forests.

Producers for People Tree

People Tree is a member of IFAT (as are most of their suppliers) – a global network of Fair Trade organisations, which is based in the Netherlands. Safia has also participated in the development of new Fair Trade organisations, setting Fair Trade standards, and she initiated World Fair Trade Day. Having been involved in this area for over 15 years she finds she is often asked for help and advice by other organisations who have found it difficult to answer the needs of the Fair Trade market. Safia spends on average two weeks travelling every month. She is based in the UK but visits Japan frequently, as she also runs the Japanese division of People Tree and Global Village. The company sources from around 70 Fair Trade organisations in 20 developing countries. Safia usually travels to Bangladesh and India every six months, and occasionally visits other countries where the company's merchandise is produced, such as Nepal and Kenya. People Tree is virtually unique amongst fashion companies in that it gives details on its website of many of the organisations which produce its garments, offering customers a transparent perspective of the way in which the company trades. Some of the producers with whom People Tree work are listed below:

Artisan Hut works with more than 250 low-income producers in Bangladesh. Many of these producers have over 20 years of experience in traditional handicrafts, with skills ranging from weaving and spinning to block printing and embroidery. Their products are created by hand and dyed without the use of harmful azo colourants. People Tree and Artisan Hut have launched a social development fund to improve the lives of these artisans and their families.

Agrocel has been supporting 180 small-scale cotton farmers in Gujarat, India and providing organic cotton for People Tree's products. Agrocel gives support to these farmers, from the selection of GM-free seeds to advice on using organic or natural pesticides. Agrocel has pioneered fair trade standards in India and now has the Fair Trade Cotton Mark. Buying organic cotton clothing helps the farmers to receive fair prices and long-term support.

People Tree's Partner, **Kumbeshwar Technical School** (KTS), based in Kathmandu, Nepal, is an educational and vocational training insititute catering to the needs of low income families. Fair Trade enables 450 women to have a stable income through hand-knitting and 250 children to receive free schooling. People Tree funds 50% of KTS's primary school expenses.

Folk Bangladesh works with approximately 550 producers in poor communities. Folk's products are made by hand and combine a wide range of traditional skills such as weaving, fabric dyeing and embroidery (see figure 7.5). Around 80% of producers are women, including a group of 40 indigenous women who are weavers living in remote areas of the country. People Tree has helped Folk to use safe and natural dyes in all the fabrics used for their garments, and supports the provision of basic health care, children's education

Figure 7.5 Traditional weaver employed by Folk Bangladesh. Courtesy of People Tree.

Cont.

Case study *Continued.*

and interest-free loans. These producers are preserving their traditional skills and providing a stable source of income for their families.

Working in Fair Trade fashion

Safia assumes the multiple roles of managing director and director of marketing, producer support and supply chain management. She works regularly with People Tree's head of PR and communication, head of design, head of producer support and financial director. The company employs eight full-time designers and technicians and a team of six people working to support producer partners. People Tree does not have a conventional buying team, so the product development and garment sourcing tasks which would usually be part of a buyer's role are shared between Safia, the designers and technicians.

Safia feels that working within a company with strong ethical principles has a huge effect on her job satisfaction. (She was recently voted one of the 50 happiest people in the UK by the *Independent* newspaper.) Her advice to anyone considering starting an ethically aware fashion company is: 'You need a lot of money. You need a lot of experience in fashion business. Ideally you'd have a lot of product development experience too'. She believes there will be 'significant growth' in the future for ethical fashion, which she says is currently growing at about 40% per year in terms of products made from organic cotton. The company has recently developed a well-publicised range for Topshop and Safia says: 'We're talking to a lot of high street people who are looking for something that really is authentic. They are coming to us to incorporate it into their product offering, or for People Tree to develop products for them.' People Tree have managed to overcome the widespread perception of ethical clothing being unattractive (see fig. 7.6), as their clothes have been worn by high-profile fashion-conscious celebrities including Sienna Miller, and the company was featured in the October 2006 edition of British *Vogue*.

The environmental stance of People Tree affects various aspects of the product development process. They work only with natural fibres, many of which are handcrafted. When buying organic cotton, buying decisions need to be made extremely early, approximately 18 months before using it in garment production. Such an early commitment to small-scale organic cotton farmers has cashflow implications for the company. Extra expense is also incurred through organic cotton certification and premium price of the yarn, as well as a fair trade premium to farmers. There is also further cost in developing new fabrics in organic cotton. Safia describes some of the more challenging aspects of sourcing products ethically:

> There still aren't many companies like People Tree. We've spent a huge amount of money developing the supply chain and there isn't yet a huge amount of funding out there to support that kind of activity. Also, there's still very little education and awareness-raising about the social and environmental impact of fashion so we find ourselves doing a lot of work in that area, which again isn't funded or subsidised, and it should be. There's a lot of documentary and media work in Japan and that hasn't yet happened in Britain.

Figure 7.6 Page from People Tree's website www.peopletree.co.uk. Courtesy of People Tree.

> If you're working with small-scale producers in isolated areas obviously their understanding of quality and tailoring is going to be reasonably low. We have spent a huge amount of energy and resources developing their skills and capacity to meet market expectations, so there's an ongoing programme of training people, of skills and capacity support building, quality management as well as paying a fair price. We bring up to 10 partners on the Market Exposure Programme to meet customers and to learn about competitive retail. This really helps. You don't expect women from a village in India to be walking around in very fitted clothes – this is a whole new dress culture to them, and it helps them to understand about consumers' expectations here in Britain.

Safia says that 'Fair Trade fashion goes beyond ethical fashion' and believes that initiatives like the ETI are important. However, as its membership is voluntary she is hopeful that changes to the law will make company directors legally accountable for their overseas activities, meeting minimum labour conditions and ideally environmental laws. Safia offers her opinion on the future of Fair Trade and sustainable fashion:

Cont.

Case study *Continued.*

It's about meeting the United Nations Millennium Development Goals, which promotes social justice within economics. Fair Trade is a tool for social development and long-term sustainability. What you'll find, hopefully in the next 10 years, is that Wal-Mart will not just be selling a few organic cotton products, but adopting handweaving communities and villages to produce Madras checks for their brand at fair prices. We'll be looking at going beyond doing the minimum and profit as the only goal. Triple bottom line that looks at financial, social and environmental benefits will become a hot topic in the fashion industry in the next five years.

Chapter 8

Buying for Own Label Fashion Multiples

Retail fashion multiples (chainstores) have numerous outlets and although they vary in terms of target market, buying systems and departmental structure, the main principles of fashion buying for multiples remain broadly the same. Within this book the fashion multiple is defined as a fashion retailer with more than twenty stores, and most have over a hundred branches. Fashion multiples dominate the clothing market in the UK and this sector contains the highest proportion of fashion buying jobs in this country. Most fashion multiples develop own label product ranges (usually referred to as 'private brands' in the USA). Compared with the UK, multiples tend to be less predominant in other European countries where there is more emphasis on independent fashion retailers selling branded merchandise.

Major UK store groups

Most fashion multiples are subsidiaries of a parent company which often has a different name from its high street stores. The domination of the UK fashion market by store groups peaked during the 1980s and 1990s, with four major parent companies owning the majority of specialist fashion stores during that era: the Burton Group, Next, Sears and Storehouse. By 2000, UK store groups had consolidated, leaving only two of these companies with a significant portfolio of stores. The Sears group (not to be confused with its American namesake) disbanded during the 1990s and its stores were sold to several different companies.

The Burton Group demerged from the department store Debenhams during the 1990s, changing its name to the Arcadia Group, and leaving Debenhams as a separate company. Arcadia retained all of the fashion chains owned by the Burton group (Top Shop, Top Man, Burton, Dorothy Perkins, Evans and Outfit) and acquired Miss Selfridge and Wallis from Sears in 1998. The fashion tycoon Phillip Green now owns the Arcadia group and Bhs. Rubicon Retail Limited now owns the former Arcadia group stores Principles and Warehouse as well as Shoe Studio Group (Bertie, Chelsea Cobbler, Nine West, Pied a Terre and Roland Cartier). Next successfully survived the 1990s with its men's, women's and children's fashion stores intact, as well as its interiors range and mail order catalogue.

Alexon and Baugur are newer contenders in the competitive UK fashion retail market. Alexon comprises the classic middle market womenswear brands Alex & Co, Ann Harvey, Dash, Eastex, Minuet and Kaliko as well as the footwear retailer Dolcis, the young fashion retailer Bay Trading and the branded menswear chain Envy. The Icelandic investment company Baugur has rapidly developed an impressive and diverse portfolio of UK fashion retailers through the acquisition of Oasis, Karen Millen, Whistles and Coast (which were named the Mosaic group in 2004) in addition to Jane Norman and MK One. Baugur also owns various food retailers and the toy store Hamleys as well as stakes in Matthew Williamson's ready-to-wear range, French Connection, House of Fraser and Woolworths plc.

In addition to specialist fashion chains several other retailers are major players in the UK led by Marks and Spencer (a variety chain) which has consistently remained the leader by turnover in the UK clothing market for many years. Marks and Spencer sells interiors products and groceries in addition to clothing and has long held a reputation for producing quality merchandise. Its total turnover for fashion-related products in 2004 was £3.4 billion, substantially outperforming its nearest rivals (Retail Intelligence, 2005). Marks and Spencer suffered from a poor media profile in the late 1990s, due to falling profits and a reduction in UK garment production, yet at the same time it remained profitable in a difficult economic climate in the retail sector. According to figures published by Key Note (2006) Next and Arcadia rank second and third respectively in terms of annual turnover of UK fashion retailers.

Finding information on store groups

It is advisable for those seeking a career in fashion buying to research into companies when job-seeking, to be aware of the range of employers available and to be well-prepared for interviews (see Chapter 12). Corporate ownership of fashion stores in the UK is subject to frequent change and it is essential for those who want to remain aware of the current structure of companies in the high street to read the trade press and quality newspapers' financial pages, or to visit fashion retailers' websites for the latest information. As this book goes to press, Rubicon Retail is rumoured to be merging with Mosaic Fashions. Some stores have been subject to numerous retail takeovers and demergers; the womenswear chain Richards once belonged to Storehouse before being sold to Sears, and is now a casualty of the ever-changing retail sector, having been completely closed down in 2000. Store groups' annual reports detail the company structure and list subsidiaries. If a store group is a public limited company (plc) annual reports are automatically available to members of the general public, often displayed in the corporate information sections on the companies' websites. Annual reports provide financial information about the parent company, including annual turnover and profit, and often contain written and visual information about the subsidiaries. Annual reports are not published separately for individual fashion retail chains within a store group and it is therefore important when researching into a store to be aware of the name of the parent company. This can be discovered simply by asking sales staff in the store or by looking at company literature such as a storecard application form.

Categories of fashion multiples

Fashion multiples can be classified into several categories, depending on the range of merchandise which is offered.

Specialist fashion multiples

As its name suggests, the specialist fashion multiple concentrates on selling fashion merchandise. Stores within this category can be classified within the following price brackets:

Lower mass market

- Bay Trading
- H&M
- Mackays
- Mark One
- Matalan
- New Look
- Peacocks
- Primark
- Select.

Middle mass market

- Arcadia group (see above)
- Adams
- Gap
- Kookai
- Mothercare
- Next
- Oasis
- River Island
- Zara.

Upper mass market

- Coast
- East
- French Connection
- Hobbs
- Jigsaw

- Karen Millen
- Monsoon
- Reiss.

This list is not exhaustive but gives an indication of stores and their direct competitors within particular price ranges. The price brackets are not absolutely definitive as fashion retailers can reposition their pricing strategies and frequently offer a selection of sub-brands with different price brackets. Stores at the lower end of the mass market were particularly successful during the late 1990s, with consumers focusing on value for money, though their dominance has abated somewhat since 2000. The middle mass market has the highest concentration of fashion multiples in the UK making it a crowded sector, though it is aimed at the largest segment of fashion consumers.

Although Karen Millen's price range is substantially higher than Monsoon's both have been classified in the upper mass market. Relatively few fashion multiples in this country occupy the ground between mass market stores and the more prestigious designer collections, which cover a wide price range, and which have been referred to as the 'masstige' market.

There is a current trend towards diversification in specialist fashion multiples by selling fashion-orientated products in addition to clothing, so Oasis sells jewellery, sunglasses, luggage, lingerie and footwear. Accordingly, buyers with experience in working with fashion products other than clothing are increasingly in demand.

Franchises

Specialist fashion multiples occasionally operate on a franchise basis, where the store is run by a franchisee, who purchases all of the products from the franchisor (the originator of the store's concept and image). The franchise contract obliges the franchisee to pay an initial start-up fee and subsequent royalties to the franchisor. This may seem a relatively expensive method of setting up a retail business, yet it could be argued that the franchise has a good chance of success from trading under an established brand name, with the overheads of range planning, product development and promotion being borne by the franchisor. Franchising is fairly rare within the UK fashion market, and is one of the modes of retail operation for the European brands Benetton, Mango and Kookai, allowing them an effective route into overseas expansion. Equally, many UK high street chains offer franchises of their stores in other countries. The advantage to the franchisor is that the retail concept can expand into new markets with the minimum of investment in stores, as well as the benefit of regular income from franchisees.

Variety chains

Variety chains are stores which sell a variety of fashion and household products, primarily under the retailer's own label. The most famous UK-based variety chain is Marks and Spencer and its main competitor is Bhs (originally called British Home Stores) which sells products at a similar price level. The market share of many middle mass market variety chains has been eroded, with Littlewoods and C&A becoming casualties of the strong competition from value retailers. Despite closing its retail outlets, Littlewoods has retained its mail order business (see Chapter 9). Woolworths is a variety chain with a unique mix of products, and although it stocks mainly household items it offers a significant amount of clothing, most notably its Ladybird range of childrenswear. Boots could also be classified within this category; though it is known largely for toiletries, it also offers childrenswear, with an emphasis on baby and toddlers' clothing, which is currently developed on their behalf by Adams (Mini Mode) and OshKosh.

Department stores

A department store is a retail outlet that sells numerous types of product, concentrating mainly on clothing and household goods. Most of the products are from a variety of brands but the department store usually also sells merchandise under its own brand. Department stores thrived as fashion retailers during the first half of the twentieth century, but declined in popularity from the 1970s with the rise of the specialist fashion multiples. There are still several major department store groups in the UK, including Debenhams, Fenwick, House of Fraser and John Lewis. These stores are renowned for their selections of fashion merchandise which often comprise a variety of price ranges, but they tend to concentrate mainly on the mass market to middle market price bracket. During the past decade, some UK department stores opened new branches, including new Harvey Nichols outlets in Leeds, Manchester and Edinburgh and Selfridges stores in Manchester and Birmingham. (Fashion-orientated department stores in major cities are listed in Chapter 4, Table 4.1.)

Most buyers for department stores select products from branded ranges (see Chapter 11). Department stores also employ buyers to develop in-house ranges which may be sold under the store's own name or under another label, for example House of Fraser's Linea and Platinum ranges. Some department stores such as Debenhams offer several of their own ranges as their stores cater for a wide range of customer types. Department stores have different buying teams for separate ranges, giving the impression of offering several different stores under one roof.

Concessions

Many department stores operate concessions where space within the store is leased to another retailer, so House of Fraser has Kookai and Levis concessions within some of its outlets. This part of the store is likely to have its own separate retail image and the sales staff are employed by the company running the concession. Traditionally the concession method has been used by middle market brands aimed at a conservative, mature market, including Jaeger, Alexon, Eastex and the Jacques Vert group: Planet, Precis, Windsmoor, Melka and Tenson, some of which also operate stand-alone stores.

Supermarkets

Supermarkets are becoming increasingly important in the UK fashion market. The major competitors in the supermarket sector are Tesco, Asda and Sainsbury's. Asda was bought by the American value retailer, Wal-Mart, in 2000, and its 'George' clothing range was subsequently launched in the USA. The success of a trial stand-alone George store in central Leeds has led to further openings of the concept within UK city centres. Sainsbury's launched a new range of clothing named 'Tu' in 2004, including childrenswear developed through Adams, replacing a collection designed by Jeff Banks.

Supermarkets benefit from having a large number of frequent customers who can be tempted to make impulse purchases of clothes whilst buying the weekly shopping, and therefore have a much higher 'footfall' of customers than most specialist fashion multiples. Supermarkets' target profit margins are lower than other mass market retailers due to high sales volume, and they can therefore offer better value in their clothing ranges than high street competitors. The buying power of Tesco has allowed the company to buy in products from the so-called 'grey market', which involves buying designer branded goods from middle-men rather than from the direct source, and selling it on to the public at much reduced prices. This has been an ongoing contentious issue as designer brands do not support this practice, since it appears to cheapen the appeal of their products, and are usually unwilling to sell directly to supermarkets.

Discount retailers

Stores within this category stock merchandise from a variety of brands at discount prices displayed by size in a minimal environment. Many of the products are bought as end-of-line ranges and others may be developed in conjunction with brands specifically for the discount retailer. The USA-based TK Maxx is the leader in this market and has expanded rapidly throughout the UK within the past decade.

Outlet stores

The American-style 'outlet village' concept arrived in the UK in the 1990s. Outlet villages are generally located in out-of-town sites in the form of purpose-built shopping centres selling a wide range of discounted designer-level, middle market and mass market products. Bicester shopping village in Oxfordshire contains stores as diverse as Monsoon and Versace. Prices are low because much of the merchandise on sale is from previous seasons or phases, and occasionally one-off development samples which are unique variations on a style are sold in outlet stores. This enables designer-level companies to retain an upmarket appearance in their standard stores, which are usually located in London, well away from the outlet village. McArthur Glen operate 16 designer outlets in the UK and Europe. There are also independent outlet villages, including Atlantic Village in Devon and Gretna Gateway Outlet Village in Scotland.

International fashion multiples

Certain fashion multiples from the USA and Europe have expanded worldwide and several have made an impact on the UK market, competing directly with home-grown fashion chains. Well known international fashion multiples include:

- Mango, Zara, Bershka, Massimo Dutti (Spain)
- Benetton (Italy)
- Kookai, Morgan (France)
- Gap (USA)
- Hennes & Mauritz (H&M) (Sweden).

Many UK fashion multiples also have overseas branches, including Marks and Spencer and Dorothy Perkins. Topshop is currently planning to launch outlets in the USA.

Factory shops

All clothing manufacturers need to dispose of seconds, which are garments of substandard quality. Many seconds are caused by poor sewing quality and others may be due to fabric faults which were not identified before garment manufacture. Manufacturers' and retailers' QC departments aim to eradicate most quality problems before garments are delivered to stores, leaving manufacturers with a certain amount of stock considered unacceptable to the original retailer and needing to be sold elsewhere to recoup some of the costs.

Clothing manufacturers often have their own factory shops which can utilise space within the building thereby generating lower overheads than renting a store in a shopping centre. Prices are therefore particularly low, often around 50% of high street prices, to account for the lower quality of the merchandise and the relatively low costs of running the shops. Premises are usually very basic which most customers expect at such low prices. Despite such shops usually being out-of-town, customers often hear of them by word-of-mouth and are willing to travel some way for the satisfaction of finding a bargain.

In the UK many factory shops used to be based around the North and Midlands where most of the country's garment manufacture was concentrated, and only a limited amount still exist. Some factory shops employ buyers who may combine the role with managing the shop, though there is obviously far less product development involved, if any, compared with buying for a high street retailer. The factory shop system operates in many different countries, including Hong Kong.

Product assortment

Retailers can offer a 'narrow and deep' or 'broad and shallow' product assortment. A narrow and deep buying policy refers to buying a relatively small number of styles in high volume. This minimises the amount of development of different products and is more efficient to manufacture in bulk. As this method is usually more cost-effective it can lead to higher profits for the companies involved and/or lower prices for the store's customers. However the production of a large quantity of the same garment results in a lack of exclusivity, which is very important to certain sectors of the fashion market. Retailers with a narrow and deep product assortment include UK chain stores focusing on classic merhandise, such as Marks and Spencer and Bhs who buy most garments in quantities of tens of thousands. In the late 1990s both of these retailers suffered from much-publicised lower profits and takeover bids, resulting in a review of their buying strategies.

Buying to a 'broad and shallow' policy means offering a wide selection of garment styles in limited numbers per style. This involves more extensive product development from the fashion buyer, thereby incurring higher costs for the retailer. The products will possibly cost more or be of a slightly lower quality standard than if they were made in larger quantities, but the customer is offered a wider choice of garments within the store. A broad and shallow policy is suitable for the younger, more design-led high street retailers such as Oasis and Top Shop, which usually buy products in quantities of a few thousand per style. As the buyer is allowed to order a wider selection of products per season, this allows the range to be constantly updated in response to changing trends. Customers realise that the availability of these products is limited, prompted by promotions such as 'Buy it before it's gone' signs in Topshop. Some retailers achieve a balance by adopting a buying policy somewhere between the two methods described above. A store such as Gap could be considered to work to a narrow and deep policy, but gives the customer a wide product choice by offering a wide range of colourways per product, particularly in womenswear.

Retail fashion multiples give their stores different classifications, dependent upon the size and location of the store and therefore the variety of products offered, for instance 'grade A' for the largest stores through to 'grade C' for the smallest branches. Smaller stores inevitably receive a narrower range of merchandise, with more of an emphasis on classic styles and a limited number of the more fashionable items.

Retail sales performance

As explained in Chapter 3 the performance of a range is often assessed by comparing current sales figures to those in the same period during the previous year, usually in terms of the amount of financial turnover. Retailers can also calculate sales per square metre of floor space within stores. This takes into account the amount of available selling space, which may have increased owing to store openings or extensions, enabling like-for-like comparisons to be made with the previous year. It is possible to adjust sales targets within a given period dependent upon the prevailing economic conditions and market activity. Sales per square metre can be calculated by the following method:

$$\frac{\text{Total sales within a chosen period}}{\text{Number of square metres in which products are sold}} = \text{Sales per square metre}$$

Calculating sales per square metre is useful for fashion multiples when assessing the profitability of merchandise where separate ranges are sold either within a store or within different stores. Such figures would enable a department store selling several brands to assess which made the most successful use of the space available. Brands which were not performing well could be replaced with new ranges or more successful brands could be extended into this space. Companies in the value sector, particularly supermarkets, benefit from a high volume of sales per square metre, generating a faster turnover of stock than many stores in the middle mass market.

Sales markdowns

During January and July most fashion stores hold their major seasonal sales in order to clear stocks ready for the new season's merchandise. Most items in sales tend to be styles where the buyer has overestimated the order quantity or price. In recent years certain retailers have begun to discount merchandise in the run-up to Christmas, traditionally the most successful selling period, reflecting the fact that some retailers face increasing competition from the lower mass market level. Additionally some stores hold mid-season sales, usually in April and October, to dispose of slow-selling lines while they are still relevant to current fashion trends and appropriate for the seasonal weather. If this merchandise were held back until the end-of-season sale the retailer would probably have to sell it at a lower price to persuade customers to purchase a style which had become out of date. The mid-season sale therefore allows garments to be sold off with the minimum reduction and the turnover from it becomes available to buy new products rather than being tied up in redundant stock. Short-term markdowns, after which garments revert to their original prices, enable retailers to boost sales within a given period. Debenhams pioneered this method with one-day, nationally-advertised 'blue cross sales', and other stores have followed their lead with discounts being offered for a limited number of days. Next takes the approach of reorganising the store format for a short time during sale periods to present reduced merchandise on long rails while the new season's full-price range is displayed in a separate section of the store. Other retailers such as Miss Selfridge have a limited amount of stock on sale at most times during the year but tend to keep this in a more discreet location at the back of the store or on the first floor level.

Visual merchandising and point-of-sale

The way in which products are displayed in stores can have a marked effect on the performance of a garment range. This is the responsibility of the visual merchandiser (VM), and the buyer is rarely directly involved in this process despite the potential impact upon sales. VMs organise the display of products on the shopfloor and in windows. Large retail chains have VM managers who produce a corporate look for all of the retailer's stores, and this is communicated to VMs to be implemented within all of the branches so that a consistent image is maintained. A store's window display is one of the key elements in enticing customers into the store. This valuable space is usually reserved for the season's key fashion items and is updated regularly. Once customers are in the store it is acknowledged that the majority of them are likely to purchase more basic products than those in the window, but the display serves its purpose by attracting the customer inside.

'Point-of-sale' (p.o.s.) promotional material is that which is displayed and distributed within stores. This includes photographs of garments which have been featured in magazines and brochures and displays promoting particular brands. Point-of-sale promotional techniques provide the retailer with the final opportunity to persuade the customer to make a purchase, at the last stage in the decision-making process. Some p.o.s. methods continue to influence the customer after leaving the store, such as leaflets, which often promote storecards which can encourage the customer's loyalty to the store, and brochures featuring the current range. These may be put into the carrier bag with a purchased item to persuade the customer to make a return visit.

Summary

Retail fashion multiples fit into the lower, middle and upper price brackets within the mass market and can be classified in several categories including:

- specialist fashion multiples
- variety chains
- department stores
- supermarkets
- outlet stores.

Retailers buy product assortments which are either narrow and deep or broad and shallow. Sales markdowns at certain times of year allow stores to remove products with poor sales figures to be replaced by new stock. Visual merchandising and point-of-sale techniques are used by retailers to maximise sales.

References and further reading

Key Note (2006) *Clothing and Footwear Industry Market Review March 2006*. Key Note, London.

Retail Intelligence (2005) *Clothing Retailing – UK July 2005*. Mintel, London.

Websites

www.alexon.co.uk
www.arcadiagroup.co.uk
www.mosaic-fashions.co.uk
www.shoppingvillages.com

CASE STUDIES IN OWN LABEL FASHION BUYING

1. Oasis

Beth Jelly is buying manager for knitwear at Oasis Stores plc. She studied on an art foundation course at Bristol Polytechnic before taking a degree in textile design at Leicester Polytechnic, specialising in knitted and woven fabrics. She started her first job as a trainee knitwear buyer for Next plc in 1985. She progressed to working as a junior buyer and then a buyer for knitwear and jerseywear in the womenswear department of Next. In 1989 Beth joined the newly formed George Davies Partnership as a buyer for knitwear and jerseywear, working on the 'George for Asda' range. In 1995 she became a buyer at Oasis for woven garments from India as well as jerseywear. Beth was promoted in 1996 to senior buyer for jerseywear, which included the initial development of the swimwear range. She then became responsible for managing the knitwear, jerseywear and swimwear buying team, comprising almost 50 per cent of the garments sold by Oasis.

Roles and responsibilities

The buying team is headed by a buying director who is responsible for three buying managers for different product types, with a team of buyers, assistant buyers (ABs) and clerks (see Figure 8.1).

The clerks are mainly graduates who can progress to AB level. The buying team works regularly with three key departments: merchandise, design and QA. Beth sits with the rest of the knitwear team in the office: two ABs and a clerk,

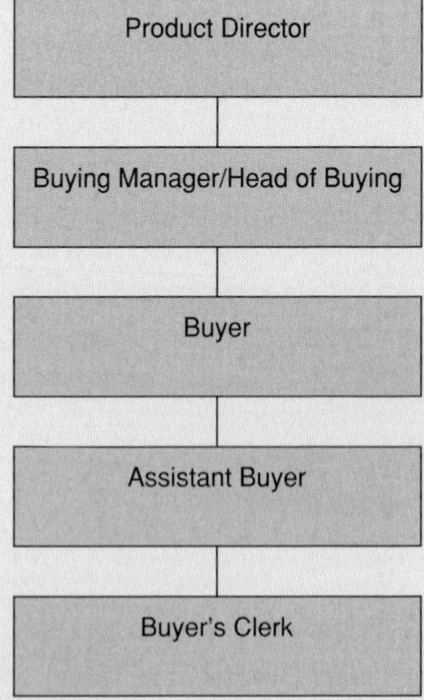

Figure 8.1 Structure of the Oasis buying department.

the merchandiser and assistant merchandiser. QA sit nearby and the designers have their own studio within the same office. Beth also has some contact with the marketing department, supplying them with garments for photo shoots and indications of products that she expects to sell well. She views working closely with her colleagues as one of the positive aspects of her job:

> I enjoy working in a team. I really enjoy developing the product and working with people internally as well as externally to get the product right. I really enjoy the fact that every day is different – there's a structure that we have to work to, but there are constantly-changing priorities so you cannot possibly get bored. You have to constantly adjust your day as things come up, which is quite frequently.

Beth's primary responsibilities are to manage the buying of the knitwear range:

> I buy the knitwear, despite being a buying manager, which is a bit unusual, because I specifically wanted to keep in touch with the product. My job is split quite equally between buying and managing. My major task is getting the right garment developed within the time. You have to negotiate and fit the garment and buy it in the right colours and quantities, but you also have to source the right suppliers and build up supplier relations. Without the right suppliers you can't do your job properly at all.

When considering working with new suppliers Beth looks for facilities or knitwear gauges, such as fine gauge, shaping or linking, to fill in gaps within the existing supply structure. To work with Oasis, manufacturers need to sell garments within a certain price and quality band. Beth frequently receives letters and telephone calls from potential new suppliers so she sends them a standard form to complete to explain how long they've been in business, their gauges, who they supply and their facilities. She also assesses the suppliers' speed and flexibility for making sample garments, and their production time:

> The shorter the time that we can turn sampling and production around, the more reactive we can be. Sometimes suppliers approach buyers directly, and once we see a supplier that we think is potentially good, we'll ask them to do some cross-costings or sampling so that we can do a like-for-like comparison. We then get our QC involved and they would do a factory check. We work with our suppliers in an honourable, loyal and respectful way. We have very good relationships with our suppliers and treat them as equal partners. We've started working with some great new factories which have canteens and creches and if anyone inspected our suppliers' factories I'd be confident that there'd be no problems.

The buying cycle at Oasis starts with an initial concept meeting where the designers present their concept boards of styling and colours for the season. The design team show the garments in 'modules', the term used by Oasis for grouping clothes as to their end use, such as casual, going out, work wear or occasion wear, to ensure that customers are not receiving a 'mixed message'.

Cont.

Case studies *Continued.*

The next stage is a department planning meeting involving buyers, designers and merchandisers. Beth describes how these meetings operate:

> There's an open discussion between buying and design and we discuss what styles and ideas they have drawn up to decide which samples or knit swatches to have made. So, from that, we'll send out specs and sketches to the suppliers we work with to request samples. Most of the designs are done in-house with a small amount of designs being developed by suppliers.

Thirty to forty per cent of the range will be sampled by manufacturers at this stage. Beth decides on appropriate selling prices and which products will be presented at the next meeting, which is 'vision day', reformulating garments with design and redrawing them if necessary. Beth explains the next stages in the selection process:

> We normally look at the products within a range for a particular season six times within a four-to-five month period in a formal meeting and we look at it every week in between that. The range we're mainly working on at a certain time will be racked in our room for us to view. The vision day is a meeting where all departments get together to see what the products in store will look like together with tears, sketches and some garment samples and inspirational ideas. Once we've done that we have a pre-selection meeting when we have most of the garment samples back from suppliers which are reasonably correct for style, fabric and colour. We do pre-selection as a whole team, where we see all of the product that will be in store for any particular month. We can see the full offer for the customer, making sure it looks relevant and right and identify whether there are any gaps.
>
> Selection meetings are then done by department, with the buyer presenting to the directors. All of the designers and buyers are involved in final selection, as well as the directors of buying and design and the merchandise controller: about 15 people. The first few meetings are driven more by the designer then, by pre-selection, buying take slightly more responsibility for it. We are about to introduce a meeting called pre-range review after selection, with the heads of buying, buying managers, buyers and designers. The merchandisers get involved for the figures side because what we want to do is to present to the directors at the range review meeting a range where there are no gaps, we're not overspent and it works as a range instore.

The Oasis buying team's next major meeting is range review where the whole buying team present the complete range to the directors, about seven weeks before the products go into store, with correct samples in correct colours. This is the team's last chance to check the range before it goes into production, when final adjustments to garments can be made and a small amount of open-to-buy is kept for quick response, or mainly high fashion items.

Beth and her team can be working on up to three seasons simultaneously, each at different stages of the buying cycle. During April, for example, the team finalise 'high summer' and 'transitional autumn' for the current year, whilst developing the October and Christmas ranges and viewing concept presentations for the following spring. Oasis stores receive new stock every week but the buyers aim to work on two-monthly selection periods as they find this more manageable. Towards the end of the selling season buyers are judged on the percentage of markdowns in their ranges, the intake margin they achieved and the department's performance against the plan each season.

Beth's job involves travelling, either on directional shopping trips or on visits to garment manufacturers:

> I travel to New York, Paris and Milan for inspirational visits and we also look at wgsn for trend inspiration. Ten years ago, I would have said that travel was one of the best things about the job. Travel is one of the things that I have to do to get the job done and I enjoy it, but I've done it for so many years now that it's not the element that I love most. The first two or three years is fantastic, but after 21 years it's not!

Beth deals mainly with manufacturers in the Far East, Italy and the UK, as these are the main sources of garments for her product area. She has also recently visited a supplier in Turkey. She finds that Hong Kong offers 'no limitations' with a diverse range of techniques for knitted garments, including a variety of gauges, embellishments, fastenings and crochet. Oasis has its own sourcing office in Hong Kong, which has helped Beth to work more effectively with suppliers from the Far East. She travels to Hong Kong and China twice a year, and explains why she buys 75–85% of her range there:

> It's mainly because of what they can produce, and also because the office out there has made it easier for us. I've managed to reduce the lead times from there, which is usually a huge hindrance for buyers. As a result of working very closely with two or three key suppliers I've managed to get lead times right down, so I'm finding now that Hong Kong is very flexible and efficient.

Beth sources up to 10% of the knitwear range from the UK and Europe though ideally she would like to buy more:

> I think they're finding business very hard, but I don't think the UK has invested in time in the right facilities for make-up, the right machinery and yarn development, and they haven't moved on fast enough, but we do try to maintain some business in Europe. I hope things will change, as delivery can be a couple of weeks quicker than from the Far East, but I find it difficult to buy from here, because it's very difficult to get the product.

Beth considers the most difficult aspect of her job to be judging what the customer will want to buy, well ahead of the selling season. She thinks that this is easier for buyers in what she describes as 'middle market mainstream retailers', who could say: 'Yes, the customer wants a turtle-neck, she had one last season, and she'll probably want a similar one with two new fashion colours'. However at Oasis the customer may really want a product for one or

Cont.

Case studies *Continued.*

two months, then no longer want it. Beth considers judging the life cycle of the product to be one of the buyer's hardest tasks as she is finding that sometimes trends are speeding up and peaking more quickly. To help with this task she describes several ways in which the buying team receives feedback from customers:

> On a Monday morning after the sales meeting, we have a meeting with feedback from the retail team for the previous week, including strengths, weaknesses, opportunities and threats. They'll talk about what competitors have done, what's out there in the high street. They give us feedback on people's windows, how we compare to them and things that they love or things that aren't quite right, like fit issues or colour issues. We also have a meeting where we review our own product areas, saying what we've done right and wrong, so that we learn for the next season. We have all the information typed with best-sellers and photographs, then we do an action plan to work to for the following season. Buyers also do store visits once or twice a season where they work in the fitting rooms, and see what customers are trying on and speak to staff. We run around and get things from the stock room, and the customers have no idea who we are.

Skills and training

Oasis offers several training courses for buyers including team-building and written skills. Numeracy and computer skills are necessary for buyers at Oasis but are not the main skills required for the job, according to Beth:

> The amount of numeracy you need depends on which company you go to. It's not my strength, to be honest. I do enough of that to make it work for the job, but it's not my driving passion for the job at all. I've managed to work in companies that are very product-led, so it's fine, but I suppose that's different in companies where the job is a little less creative, so you need to pick the retailer that's right for you. The buyers at Oasis assess the profitability of the range from budgets and targets. The buyers have a set target margin for their ranges, which they aim to maintain. We use computers for e-mailing, internally and to suppliers. Buying and design probably use computers the least.

Oasis began to offer internet shopping in 2006, their website having been previously used only for promotional purposes. Beth is keeping a watchful eye on the market. The company's closest competitor is considered to be Warehouse, with many customers aspiring to shop at stores in a higher price bracket such as Karen Millen and French Connection. Beth also expects River Island and Top Shop customers to aspire to shopping at Oasis.

Recruitment

Oasis is one of four womenswear brands in the Mosaic portfolio. Oasis was the first brand in the group, acquiring Coast in 1998. Following a secondary management buyout in November 2003, Mosaic acquired Karen Millen and

Whistles in June 2004. The creative teams are based in one office building in central London, with each of the brands operating from a different floor. Whilst the creative teams work completely independently, there are opportunities for employees to progress into jobs in sister companies within Mosaic.

For level one assistant buyers or clerks Oasis recruits either from colleges or via an agency. Applicants do not necessarily have to be graduates. For senior ABs, who need prior experience, the human resources department refers to application letters which are kept on file or approach an agency. Applicants go through an initial interview followed by a second interview with a presentation on a product area or project for Oasis. They may then be called in for a third interview, particularly for a senior position. Of Oasis's six buyers and buying managers, only two have a fashion degree. Beth offers the following advice for anyone wishing to pursue a career in buying:

> The others have either worked their way up through the business, or they've done marketing, so it means you don't need to have a fashion degree. We look for people with drive, who can work well with a team, have good communication skills and obviously a good eye for fashion. Focus on what you want to do before you leave college, as early as you can in your final year – don't leave it until afterwards. If you can, do a sandwich course. I didn't do it, but it counts for a lot with retailers when they employ people, because they have someone on board that they know and they can take on when they leave college. If you think you want to do buying, don't take anything else, don't get side-tracked. If people really want to do buying, they've got to keep approaching people. If you're right, you'll get there in the end.

2. Jaeger

Zarina Kanji has been a buying assistant at Jaeger for 18 months, based in their head office in central London, since graduating with a first class honours degree in Fashion Marketing and Communication from Nottingham Trent University. Established in the UK as a retailer in 1884, Jaeger now have womenswear and menswear outlets located in the UK, Europe, South America, the Middle East and the Far East.

Role and responsibilities

Zarina's key responsibilities are to manage the critical path and to solve any production issues for styles which have been bought by Jaeger. She describes the main functions of her role as:

- negotiating prices with suppliers
- ensuring all garment components are ordered and on time
- placing purchase orders with garment suppliers
- ensuring samples are sealed on time
- ensuring deliveries from suppliers are on time
- ensuring the fit of the garments is of a Jaeger standard
- being aware of Jaeger's competitors on the high street
- researching trends
- administration for the team
- maintaining the product showroom
- creating a commercial collection for the customer
- analysing sales figures and profits
- increasing profit for the company.

Zarina is usually working on two seasons' garment ranges simultaneously. She works with merchandising, QA and Cloth and Trims departments on a daily basis. She has regular weekly meetings with merchandising and QA to monitor the critical path and the progress of production sampling. Merchandisers create option plans for the buying team to work from when selecting ranges and jointly analyse the successes and failures of the collection. QA offer technical guidance to enable the buyers to achieve the look they want, and to achieve the perfect fit for the customer by fitting garments on a model. Jaeger has its own design team who collaborate with buying on the design and selection of garment styles, yarn, fabric and trims. Jaeger is in the rare position for a retailer of having its own department to source fabric and trims, the legacy of its historic past as a manufacturer. The cloth buyer develops and sources new fabrics and prints exclusive to Jaeger to ensure they are unique on the high street (see Figure 8.2).

During her first year in the job Zarina visited Portugal to meet suppliers face-to-face and discuss garment production. Daily communication with suppliers is essential for Zarina and she finds that visiting them helps to assist in understanding the way they perform. Assistant buyers at Jaeger travel to European and UK factories and certain trade fairs. Senior buyers in the company

Figure 8.2 Jaeger Black collection autumn/winter 2006. Photograph courtesy of Jaeger.

(see figure 8.3) travel twice a year to the Far East to visit suppliers, to the major European trade shows such as PV and Pitti Filati and on directional shopping trips to New York.

Zarina has annual performance reviews with her line manager to discuss how she is working. When asked about the most enjoyable and challenging aspects of her job she says:

> I enjoy the creative side – getting to approve trims and lab dips and attending fit sessions. The price negotiation and achieving on-time deliveries are also satisfying when suppliers meet targets. You have to log everything and know your delivery dates, or you're not going to have a collection. You have to hound your suppliers to get things in on time. It's important to understand the critical path because it's really baffling at first. It is difficult in the entry-level stages of the role as it is very administrative and is harder to make interesting. However the more attention and work you put into the tracking, the more rewarding and less stressful it becomes.

Zarina is responsible for chasing up garment samples for the Jaeger press shows, where the collections are presented to the fashion press prior to the launch of the products in store. She also attends the twice-yearly store managers' conference at the Royal Academy. She is involved in comparative shopping to maintain awareness of Jaeger's competitors which include Maxmara, Aquascutum, John Lewis and Hobbs. The newly-introduced Jaeger London range competes with more fashion-forward brands such as DKNY, Joseph and Zara. The buying team receive information about Jaeger customers from

Cont.

Case studies *Continued.*

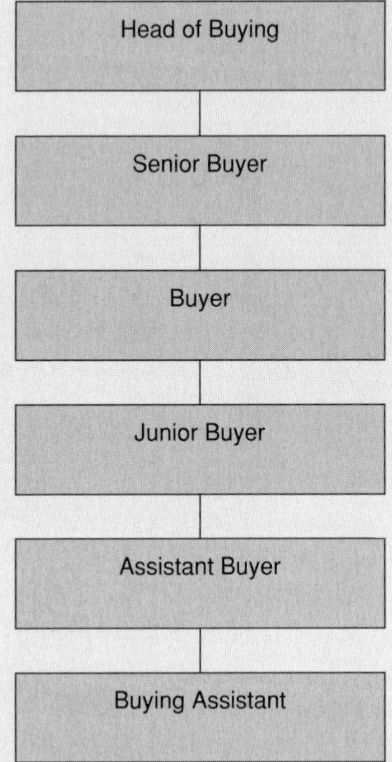

Figure 8.3 Structure of the buying department at Jaeger.

focus groups, and Zarina explains other ways in which they receive customer feedback:

> Through our 'Support a Store' scheme every member of Head Office is allocated a store to visit once a season to talk to the store manager and retail staff and gain invaluable feedback from the people who sell face-to-face to our customers. We also find out a lot about what our customers like from sales figures and in a broader sense from reaction to press coverage.

Skills and training

Zarina has participated in various training courses whilst working for Jaeger: using Microsoft Excel, 'Understanding Leather' at the British Leather Centre and 'Introduction to Garment Production' at London College of Fashion. She describes computer skills as essential within her job, as she uses MicroExcel, Word and Outlook on a daily basis (though she says that advanced knowledge of these programs is not necessary for those in entry-level roles). The main product database used by the buying team is unique to Jaeger so the staff are trained in this in the workplace. Zarina explains the skills she considers vital for a career in buying:

> Without a sound grasp of figures you cannot be aware of whether you are paying a good price for a garment and if you will make a profit, which is ultimately what a business needs to succeed. I think it is good to know what a critical path is about and to be able to understand the fundamental skills required and the main requirements of the job role when you first start. Specific jargon is quickly learnt once you are in a head office environment and people are always willing to help and explain.

Career advice

Zarina advises applicants for fashion buying jobs to gain work experience as she says 'the reality is often quite different from the idea'. Here she describes why working part-time in fashion stores between terms whilst she was a student was helpful to her career:

> I worked at Debenhams and Monsoon which provided a really good basic understanding of the way retailers operate in terms of collections, capsule ranges that fit together and how accessories complement outfits. At Debenhams I was also responsible for analysing best and worst sellers every week to look at why they were or were not selling.

She defines the qualities Jaeger look for when employing buying assistants as:

- being enthusiastic and 'on the ball'
- having an interest in fashion
- having retail awareness
- being well organised
- being willing to learn.

Chapter 9

Mail Order Fashion Buying

Fashion buying for a mail order company is very similar to the buyer's role in a retail fashion multiple, but there are distinct differences in the way in which the products are sold, impacting upon range selection and sales figures. Listed below are some of the differences between buying for mail order and retail outlets:

- It is particularly important that garments are supplied on time or customers will be disappointed: in retail, customers may not realise if garments are out of stock.
- Garments cannot be touched or seen closely by the customer before they are ordered.
- Garments often vary in colour and quality from the catalogue photograph, due to printing processes, or because they have been made in different fabrics or by different suppliers.
- Sales per page and per catalogue are calculated as a measure of the range's performance.
- The garment returns rate is much higher in mail order than in retail, largely because customers may order several garments before making a purchase decision.

Mail order buyers working on own label ranges follow a very similar buying cycle to the one described in Chapter 3. The mail order buyer's job can involve additional responsibilities to those of a retail buyer, in that they may be consulted during the compilation of the catalogue by other departments. After final selection the photo shoot takes place during the product development phase of the range. It is still possible for the buyer to make certain amendments to own label products at this stage, for example changing the length of a style, as digital imaging techniques have been developed to adapt photographs. Many mail order companies include, or focus exclusively on, branded merchandise (see Chapter 10). Mail order buyers may therefore concentrate on either own label or branded products, or occasionally both.

The mail order fashion market

Home shopping is the term used to describe mail order catalogues, online retailers and TV channels. According to Mintel (2005) the UK is Europe's second largest home shopping market and was worth £10.5 billion in 2003, with average sales of £176 per person. Many 'bricks and mortar' retailers (i.e. those with stores) also sell fashion ranges through home shopping.

Major companies in the UK mail order fashion market are:

- Littlewoods Shop Direct Group (Abound, Additions Direct, Choice, Great Universal, Kays, Littlewoods, LX, Marshall Ward, Sport-E)
- Next Directory
- Freemans (a division of Otto Versand)
- Grattan (a division of Otto Versand)
- Empire (a division of international mail order group Redcats, owned by PPR).

Until the late 1980s, most mail order companies in the UK had a reputation for focusing on conservative garment designs at the cheaper end of the market. Customers tended to work as agents by showing a catalogue such as Great Universal to friends, and earned a small commission on sales. As well as garments, the catalogues sold a wide variety of household merchandise. The products usually cost slightly more than comparable high street products but customers could spread out the payments over several months, enabling them to purchase goods which might otherwise be unobtainable to them. These so-called 'Big Book' catalogues still exist and are constantly updated to reflect a wide customer base, including sections which are bought as separate 'shops', ranging from young contemporary fashion to classic styles. Household goods, also referred to as hard goods, form a large section of these catalogues, containing products which are usually bought in a separate department from that of the fashion buying team.

The world's largest mail order company is Otto Versand, a private company based in Germany, which publishes catalogues throughout the world, including Spiegel (USA), Grattan (UK), Trois Suisses (France) and Otto (Germany). The UK's largest mail order company is Littlewoods Shop Direct Group, formed in 2005 from a merger between Littlewoods and GUS (previously known as Great Universal Stores). Freemans catalogue is one of few to be based in London: most of the major UK catalogues are based in the North, including Littlewoods (Liverpool), Grattan (Bradford) and Empire (Leeds). Most of the major mail order companies in the UK are members of the Mail Order Traders Association and adhere to its code of practice in the way that they trade.

Shopping channels Ideal World (based in Peterborough) and QVC (based in London) which sell fashion merchandise amongst other products, have become established on satellite, cable and freeview TV in the UK. Increasing penetration in the UK market of these TV formats offers potential increases in sales growth for shopping channels. Shopping channels employ buyers to select products to feature in their programmes. QVC (founded in the USA in 1986) was the first shopping channel to be launched in the UK in 1993 and employs a 'vendor relations team' to assess the suitability of products to be

Figure 9.1 Page from the first edition of Next Directory 1988. Photograph courtesy of Next.

sold on the channel. Next is expected to be the first UK high street retailer to sell its merchandise through TV, according to press reports that it would trial sales through Ideal World in 2006.

The UK mail order market was revolutionised in 1988 with the launch of the Next Directory (see Figure 9.1). Next launched an innovative store concept and fashion product range in 1982, and the Next image had an impact on store design, visual merchandising and the coordination of high street womenswear ranges. Next Directory had a similar effect on the mail order market by offering slick, minimal presentation and aspirational styling for menswear and womenswear. Most of the garments were the same as those sold through Next retail outlets, but the concept appealed to those with little time for shopping, particularly the continually increasing number of working women. There were four major differences between the new Next Directory and the traditional Big Book catalogue:

(1) The Directory was hard-backed, giving it more of a desirable coffee-table book appearance. As a result, customers were asked to pay a cover charge of £3. Although this covered a fraction of the actual cost, it made the catalogue seem more valuable and prestigious than its competitors.

(2) Delivery was promised within 48 hours by courier or post. The majority of merchandise was delivered on time, and usually more quickly than its competitors, many of whom subsequently reduced their delivery times. (Next now usually deliver products the following day.)

(3) Fabric swatches were included, to enable customers to see the colour and texture of the fabric. This system was later abandoned, as it was difficult to obtain sufficient bulk fabric at the publishing stage.

(4) Customers were not expected to operate as agents, and no commission was offered. A standard delivery charge was added to each order, rather than the 'free' delivery offered by competitors.

These factors combined with a commercial garment range, to give the Next Directory a more upmarket image than its predecessors. Mail order operations expertise was bought in by Next, by the merger with Grattan plc prior to the launch of the Next Directory. The success of the Next Directory is confirmed by the fact that the format remains largely unchanged, and Next continued to be a profitable concern during the late 1990s, at a time when many other established fashion retailers were suffering financially. Next products are now sold via retail outlets, mail order and the internet (www.next.co.uk), and garments from the catalogue can be delivered either to a home address or local store.

Compiling a catalogue

In addition to the selection of merchandise, there are numerous other processes involved in the compilation of a mail order catalogue, mostly relating to photography and publication. Buyers of mail order ranges are not likely to be involved directly with these processes but it is useful to be aware of them as they have an influence on product sales. The main processes are listed in Figure 9.2 and the roles which contribute to the compilation of the catalogue are explained below.

Art direction

It is the job of the art director to coordinate photographic shoots. Art directors are often freelance, as the job requires working for intermittent periods. Art directors have an equivalent role in mail order to that of visual merchandisers in retail fashion multiples. They have overall responsibility for the layout and image of the catalogue, which have a large influence on sales. The art director chooses the shoot location, models, stylist and photographer for the photographic shoot. The mail order buyer relies on the professionalism of the art director to enhance sales figures for the range. Buyers may have an opportunity to influence the shoot, and occasionally may attend. After the garment range has been finalised at the range presentation the fashion buyer usually briefs the art director, who sketches a plan of the layout of garment and text on

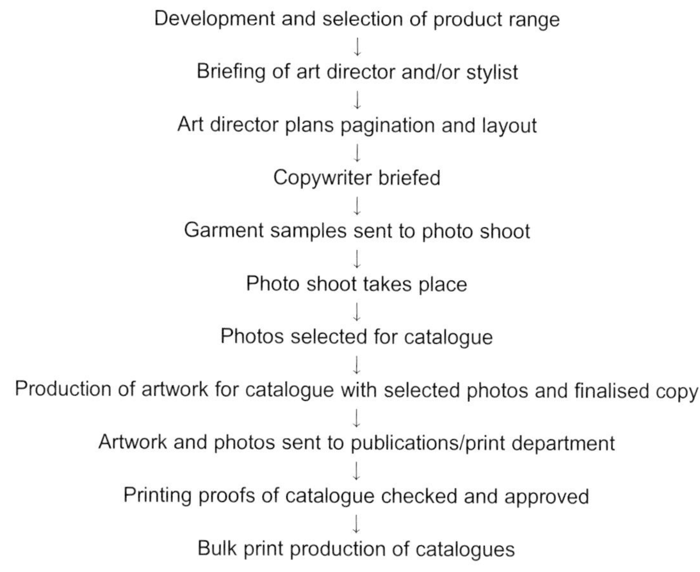
Development and selection of product range
↓
Briefing of art director and/or stylist
↓
Art director plans pagination and layout
↓
Copywriter briefed
↓
Garment samples sent to photo shoot
↓
Photo shoot takes place
↓
Photos selected for catalogue
↓
Production of artwork for catalogue with selected photos and finalised copy
↓
Artwork and photos sent to publications/print department
↓
Printing proofs of catalogue checked and approved
↓
Bulk print production of catalogues

Figure 9.2 Processes involved in the compilation of a mail order catalogue.

the catalogue pages. This is known as pagination. The buying and/or design department may also be involved in the pagination of the range. The mail order fashion buyer can use pagination as the starting point for the planning of the range, with notes and/or sketches of the layout of each page and its contents, so that each item is seen in the context of the garments with which it will be displayed in the catalogue. If the company has retail outlets as well as a catalogue, magazine editorial-style photos may be taken during the shoot for use as backdrops in window displays, or instore to promote the range.

The buyer is responsible for ensuring that the right garments are sent to the photo shoot on time. This normally takes place before bulk garment production, so the garments worn by models are samples made in manufacturers' design departments. The fit of the garment will probably not have been approved at this stage, as photo shoots often take place within a very short timescale after the final range selection. The buyer may brief the art director and/or the stylist prior to the shoot, to explain the required look of each garment. Buyers attach a label to each garment containing relevant details such as reference numbers and any special instructions. This is one of the most hectic times of the season, and the buying team must support each other and pay great attention to detail: any mistakes made during a photo shoot are likely to be costly. The garments and relevant accessories are carefully packed into boxes by the buying team, to be sent to the photo shoot. Inevitably at least one garment arrives late, which may then need to be sent to the shoot by courier from the buying office or possibly directly from the manufacturer. This is acceptable for a small number of items if they are not planned for photography on the first day of the shoot, but it would be too costly for the whole range to be sent by courier.

Photography shoots usually take place in hot climates, to improve the chances of the clothes being photographed in good lighting conditions. Popular locations therefore include Florida and South Africa. Although the background scenery may barely be noticed by the catalogue customer, the weather has an effect on the appearance of the garments and models and the overall mood of the shot. There is however no absolute guarantee of good weather and shoots sometimes need to be extended because of adverse conditions, ranging from rain to hurricanes. To accommodate late arrival of photo samples and unpredictable climates, studio shoots with models or still-lives (where garments are shown unworn) in the UK can be used as a fallback, without greatly affecting customers' demand for the products. Held options are pages shot on location or in the studio at the latest possible date, after the main shoot, enabling buyers to select products in response to fashion trends.

Fashion styling and photography

Most fashion stylists work on a freelance basis, and are responsible for achieving the appropriate image for the range at the photo shoot. This involves briefing the hairstylist and make-up artist, ensuring that the garment appears to fit correctly (often by using pins, sellotape and bulldog clips which are unseen in the photograph) and accessorising the models appropriately. The job also includes buying or hiring appropriate accessories and props such as furniture for photo shoots. The fashion stylist Tracey Jacob is a former buyer who specialises in childrenswear shoots for mail order companies, retailers and magazines. Tracey says of her job:

> My responsibilities are to work with the art directors on ideas for the shoot and come up with stories for each section of the catalogue. Communication skills are hugely important. You have to be able to voice your ideas and opinions with the photographer. It's a very important relationship and you need to be on the same wavelength with regard to images and ideas . Teamwork on a shoot is very important, especially on the actual shoot day. You have to have the right team and everyone's role is equally important to make the shoot go smoothly. Creativity is the most important skill you need for styling as without it, it's impossible to do this job well and have a good reputation. Styling is not as glamorous as you think – it's hard work with a lot of great opportunities.

During the photo shoot the team works closely together overseen by the art director. Polaroids are taken by the photographer before each shot, to give the art director an insight into how each photograph is likely to look, allowing changes to be made by the stylist and models if necessary. Photo shoots cost relatively large sums of money as they employ a team of highly-paid professionals (of which models and photographers are the most expensive) plus travel and accommodation. Several shots are taken of each pose, to allow the best image to be selected. For a mail order shoot it is essential that the garment details and fabric are photographed with enough clarity for the customers to be able to make purchasing decisions, as opposed to magazine fashion shoots, where a general mood of the clothing is being created without the need to sell products. Fashion photographers, stylists and models can often work for both mail order and magazine clients to gain sufficient income and to enjoy a variety of creative jobs, adapting their skills as necessary.

Selection of photographs

The photographs are developed as transparencies and then shown to the art director who makes a decision on the final shot to be used in the catalogue. The buyer may also be involved in the final selection of transparencies. This can be a difficult decision and requires a discerning eye as there are likely to be minor imperfections in many of the shots; the model's eyes may be partially closed or a key feature of the garment slightly obscured, which could result in lower sales. Some imperfections can be improved by the publications department by recolouring or deleting areas prior to the printing process. Digital photography and computer photo-editing programs may also allow the manipulation of images to achieve the desired effect.

Catalogue layout

It is important that the buyer has some say in the layout of the catalogue as the location and size of a photograph usually has a direct effect on sales figures. Garments on the right-hand page, products with large photographs and merchandise positioned in key positions such as the front or back cover or by the order form, usually have higher sales than products on left-hand pages or in small photographs, because the customer has higher exposure to these images. Yet if a garment is particularly appealing to the customer it will probably still sell well whatever the photograph's size or location. Equally, inappropriate garments cannot be guaranteed higher sales even if the photographs are large or well-located.

Copywriting

The written details, or copy, displayed alongside the photographs in the catalogue, may be written either by the buyer, or a professional copywriter. The copy usually comprises a brief garment description, fibre content of the fabric, available sizes and selling price. Each catalogue has its own house style for copy including the typeface used and either basic or more descriptive garment details. Other written information is also likely to be required on each page, such as a name for the range, promotional information and brand logos for either garments or fabrics. The inclusion of the phone number for orders on the page is advantageous, even though it also appears on the order form and cover, as it makes ordering easier for the customer and can therefore increase sales. The art director receives the written information and images of the logos. After scanning in the final garment photos the art director can then use the computer to mock up the pages of the catalogue prior to printing. The buyer may be asked to check the pages at this stage, allowing any necessary adjustments to be made, such as selecting a different transparency or amending details of fibre content if necessary. The finished artwork is then passed to the publications department, who brief the printers. Copies of the pages at various stages in the printing process are submitted to the publications department, and the buyer may be responsible for checking the content.

Printing and publication

Mail order companies usually have a specialist publications department (sometimes referred to as 'repro') responsible for coordinating the printing of the catalogue after the layout has been designed and finalised by the art director. Various photographic and printing processes can distort colours from the originals. Photography shoots tend to take place in warm climates or in brightly lit studios which can cause fabrics to look paler than they appear in natural daylight. Printing inks can also cause visible colour variations.

It is obviously important that catalogues show the colours of garments as realistically as possible to avoid disappointment from customers when they order the product. To ensure that the garments in the catalogue appear as close to the actual colour as possible, the publications department may request swatches of fabric or yarn from buyers for each style in the correct shade, prior to the catalogue being printed. The publications department may be responsible for checking colour-matching, or the buyer may be asked to approve initial prints of the catalogue in full colour (chromalins) by comparing them to swatches. This usually takes place under the 'natural daylight' setting of a lightbox, which is kept in a darkened room to avoid contamination from other sources of light.

Forecasting and assessing the sales performance of a mail order range

There are several ways of showing sales figures for mail order. They can be calculated either through financial turnover, total *price* of garments sold, or the total *number* of garments sold. A garment costing £50 which has sold 1000 pieces has a higher sales turnover (£50 000) than one costing £20 which has sold 2000 pieces (£40 000).

The gross sales figure for a style is the total number of garments ordered by customers multiplied by its selling price. The net sales figure denotes gross sales minus returns, showing orders which have resulted in garments being kept by customers, and is therefore the most important indicator of the sales performance of a mail order range.

The rate of returns is relatively high in mail order, often in excess of 50% of orders, largely due to customers having ordered a selection of goods and deciding which ones to keep upon receipt. Customers may simply have changed their minds on receiving the garments, or ordered several garments with the intention of buying only the best ones. As with retailers, some returns are due to quality and fit. For example upon inspection the make-up quality may not be of the standard expected by the customer, the colour may vary from the printing in the catalogue and the garment proportion may not reflect the image shown in the original photograph. This calculation can be applied either to individual garments or to a complete range:

Gross sales value – Total value of returns = Net sales

Calculating profit as a percentage of net sales gives senior managers the opportunity to compare like-for-like sales between buyers, using the following formulae:

Net sales – Total cost price of goods = Gross margin

$$\frac{\text{Net sales} - \text{Total cost price of goods}}{\text{Net sales}} \times 100 = \text{Percentage gross margin}$$

Preview catalogues, featuring a limited selection of a new season's range, can be sent to a certain amount of a mail order company's best customers in advance, to gain invaluable feedback on the possible sales performance of the range. Preview catalogues usually entice these customers to make orders by offering a discount on orders, thus offering a reward for loyalty and an incentive to provide the company with data on potential bestselling styles and poor performers. This helps merchandisers to anticipate demand for products and to buy reasonably realistic quantities for individual styles. A drawback of preview catalogues is that they are issued much earlier than the launch date of the main catalogue and the weather may affect customers' purchasing decisions. Merchandisers aim to correct this by incorporating a 'drift factor', based on sales patterns from previous years, to allow for various seasonal factors for certain products, for example beachwear and Christmas gifts. Mail order companies with their own stores can also use preview sales information to assist in estimating the quantities they order for the retail side of the business.

Buying for the internet

Fashion buying for the internet has much in common with buying for a mail order catalogue. Selling products via an internet website is known as e-commerce and companies which operate transactional websites are referred to as e-tailers. By 2000 many fashion retailers had set up websites initially for promotional purposes, many of which have now been transformed into transactional operations. Most mail order companies now sell via the internet as well as through catalogues since the two methods of distribution are complementary, based on selling from photographs, stocking merchandise at a central location and postal delivery. Next is currently the UK's largest online clothing retailer and Britain's largest online transactional website for all product types is

Tesco.com (Mintel, 2005). Its fellow bricks-and-mortar retail group Arcadia (see Chapter 8) launched its 'Zoom' website in 1999, as an internet portal, offering products from its retail fascias. This was promoted by offering free CD-Roms via its retail outlets, with free internet access. Mail order companies can find that their websites bring in new business, rather than poaching sales from their catalogues or retail outlets, owing to the different demographic profile of internet users. Websites can increase their traffic, and therefore sales volume, by creating links from affiliate websites, who earn commission from new customers' orders. The internet arm of its business had captured 45% of Next Directory's sales in 2006, with 2149 million active customers (Wolfson, 2006). The convenience for new and existing customers of being able to buy online 24 hours a day can obviously boost internet sales figures, rather than restricting shoppers to the opening times of stores or call-centres.

Companies which only sell their products online have become known as 'pure players'. Boo.com, an e-tailer specialising in branded fashion goods, was launched in a blaze of publicity in 1999, and was the victim of an equally well-publicised demise in 2000 when the company's financial backers withdrew their funds. Even the largest bricks-and-mortar retailers can profit from alliances with online pure players, as demonstrated by the following statement issued to the press in 2005 by Marks and Spencer's Director of Marketing and E-Commerce, Steven Sharp:

> Marks & Spencer already has a successful website with over 24 million visits every year, but our e-commerce and customer ordering capabilities have yet to reach their full potential. A partnership with Amazon will help us achieve this, while allowing us to concentrate on our core business of retailing.

Though the leading websites in the UK benefit from being connected to an existing retail or mail order infrastructure, a number of fashion e-tailers have established successful businesses selling exclusively online, some of which are listed in Table 9.1.

Table 9.1 Online specialist fashion businesses.

E-tailer's website address	Main business activity
asos.com	Own label menswear and womenswear ranges in the style of celebrities (see case study at end of chapter)
figleaves.com	Women's and men's branded underwear, nightwear, swimwear and sportswear
net-a-porter.com	Ready-to-wear menswear, womenswear, footwear, accessories and bags from international designer collections. Online magazine
peopletree.co.uk	Ethically-sourced fair trade menswear, womenswear and childrenswear (see case study in Chapter 7 Garment Sourcing)
yoox.com	Discount ready-to-wear menswear, womenswear, accessories, footwear, bags, jewellery, watches, underwear and gifts (based in Bologna, Italy)

With increasing access to the internet and a governmental policy of encouraging wider ownership of computers, the internet is likely to become one of the major methods of distributing fashion merchandise in the near future, following similar development processes to those used for mail order.

Summary

Buying a fashion range for mail order is largely similar to buying for a retailer, with only a few key differences. The home shopping market includes transactional websites and TV shopping channels. After final range selection, the following processes take place in the compilation of a catalogue:

- handover of sample garments to art directors and stylists
- planning of the catalogue's layout by the art director
- photo shoot
- selection of photos for the catalogue
- finalisation of catalogue layout
- printing of catalogues.

Net sales figures are used to assess the sales performance of a home shopping range. Buying for the internet is similar to buying for mail order, and this is becoming an increasingly popular method of distribution for fashion merchandise.

References and further reading

Mintel (2005) *Home Shopping Market March 2005.* Mintel, London.

Sharp, S. (2005) Marks and Spencer and Amazon Services Europe Announce E-Commerce Agreement at www2.marksandspencer.com/thecompany/mediacentre/pressreleases/2005/com2005-04-19-01.shtml

Wolfson, S. (2006) Chief Executive's review order.next.co.uk/aboutnext/companyresults/Jul2006.asp

mota.org.uk

www.redcats.com/english/redcats/index.htm

www.thecatalogshop.co.uk/catalogue-history/mail-order.php

CASE STUDIES IN MAIL ORDER FASHION BUYING

1. Boden

Suzi Avens is Womenswear Senior Buyer for wovens and accessories at Boden, the mail order fashion company (see Figure 9.3). After taking four A levels and a one-year foundation course in Art and Design, Suzi completed a BA (Hons) Fine Art degree. Her buying career began at Bhs where she worked for two years, first as a buyer's administrator then as assistant buyer for womenswear. She joined Boden six years ago and has worked in the womenswear buying teams for accessories, wovens, jersey and knitwear.

The company's clothing catalogue was launched in 1991 by Johnnie Boden, a former stockbroker. He was inspired while working in New York by American retail and mail order companies for the 30-something customer. He decided to change career completely by establishing a similar type of mail order company in the UK, on a much smaller scale, developing clothes which would appeal to him and his friends. He started with a menswear range, and introduced womenswear three years later, followed by the Mini Boden childrenswear range.

Role and responsibilities

Suzi describes her main responsibilities as:

Figure 9.3 Suzi Avens of Boden visiting a garment manufacturer.

- being an inspirational leader for the buying teams
- ensuring everyone in the team is clear on shared goals and motivated to do their best to meet and exceed them
- constantly looking ahead to pre-empt problems and improve processes
- building a team which is efficient and effective
- selecting and buying a great range which Boden customers love
- ultimately producing a range which meets and exceeds targets whilst delivering excellent customer satisfaction through service, quality, design, colour, details etc.

Suzi works very closely with the company's merchandising, garment technology and design teams on a daily basis. She explains how she collaborates with various colleagues within the company:

> We liaise regularly with other departments (mini and menswear) to discuss their strategies and in turn the company's strategy. For example, before we decide to place a certain number of styles with a supplier, we will review the business growth for that supplier as a company rather than in isolation. Also we work closely with the catalogue photography teams, deciding which styles will share a page, which colours will be photographed, what the end use/feel of the photo will be, what details we want shown etc. With the graphic design team we discuss layouts/fonts/copy etc. And we spend time with the shop and warehouse understanding how they work, listening to their comments and how our decisions affect them and helping them out when they are busy, such as during the sale.

Suzi enjoys many aspects of her role, particularly 'the fact each day is different' and 'the satisfaction of the team meeting and exceeding its objectives'. She says some of her favourite parts of the job include working with the team, problem solving, thinking on her feet and the selection/design process as well as facing challenges and new situations. Analytical skills are essential to enable her to understand more about the company's customers, improve current processes and to analyse sales figures. However she thinks that the parts of the job people like can vary because 'every element has its challenges and every individual will have different elements they struggle with or find easy'.

Like most buyers, Suzi usually works on three seasons of merchandise simultaneously. Whilst the summer 2006 sale is being traded she is reviewing the photography for the autumn/winter 2006 catalogue and deciding whether to place more orders, ensuring deliveries will be on time and managing quality queries from the warehouse from delivered stock. Suzi describes the other tasks she is involved in during the same period:

> We review the preview sales for the next season by emailing an early web link to selected customers to get a read on sales. We are constantly thinking about future ranges and if we need to tweak them in light of these sales. Spring/Summer 2007 styles which will be in our range have now been confirmed and we are finalising prices and approving lab dips for them. All fabrics have been wearer-trialled but now we will be ordering wearer trials of every style to

Cont.

Case studies *Continued.*

check the shape/design works. Fitting sessions have started and critical path dates are being sent to suppliers, which we review as a team on a weekly basis. We will start to think about Autumn/Winter 2007 in a few weeks, firstly focusing on fabrics, reviewing our current fabrics in conjunction with returns to decide if we need to upgrade/change/consolidate etc., and then looking for new fabrics to develop where needed.

Suzi's job involves travelling to a variety of locations during the buying cycle. Each season she goes to Paris for PV and directional shopping, Florence for Pitti Filati and the Spin Expo yarn show in Shanghai. The buyers don't do many directional shopping trips as this is part of the design function at Boden. However, the buying team keep up to date through shopping trips in London and assessing trends in fashion magazines. Suzi also visits suppliers and factories in Europe and the Far East, usually twice a year, to run through new designs and ideas for the forthcoming season and she says: 'We also spend time with everyone involved in the process of making our garments ensuring they understand our customer, brand and our requirements.'

Skills and training

Boden offer buyers a variety of internal training courses such as motivational leadership and ethical trading. Suzi and her colleagues also attend external courses where relevant, which are more specific in content, for example understanding knitwear and sourcing strategy. Suzi emphasises the importance of teamwork within the company: 'It's absolutely critical. We work as a team all the time. For example we have a weekly buying meeting where we run through everyone's workloads and who needs to help who to achieve our shared goals.'

Performance is assessed at Boden in twice-yearly appraisals and one-to-one meetings between employees and managers at least once a month. Suzi conducts appraisals for her team (see Figure 9.4) and she says: 'We do spend quite a bit of time on each individual, making sure they understand and agree with their objectives'. The buying team gain knowledge of their target customers through focus groups and what Suzi describes as: 'customer watching – visiting places we know a lot of Boden people visit such as fairs/shops/parks etc., interviewing customers and spending time working in the shop and call centre'.

Career advice

Suzi did placements before becoming a buyer, including graphic design, interior design and working in the fashion department of a magazine. She says:

> I researched into fashion buying so much I had a pretty clear idea of what the job was about before I started. I gained a wide variety of work experience to make sure the first job I took was totally 'me'. I also spent a lot of time reading up on jobs and speaking to anyone and everyone I knew in a creative job.

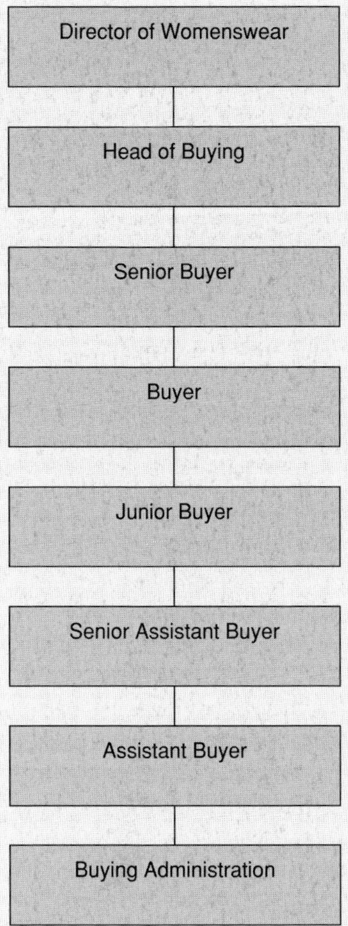

Figure 9.4 Structure of the Boden womenswear buying department.

Although in some companies most buyers have done a fashion course, it is not always the case. In fact, some of the best buyers I know, both at Boden and at other companies, didn't do one. However, we do look for people who have a degree and amongst other skills, a creative flair. Being interested in fashion is a great start but there are many more skills needed to be a great buyer. If you are open to learning and challenges and don't think you know it all it's a good start! It's hard work and you need to be prepared to get your hands dirty and work long hours. But it's also lots of fun!

Suzi advises researching and preparing before sending a covering letter and CV and attending an interview. She adds:

Tweak your CV if needed as every job and company is different, and if you show you know that you will be much more likely to get an interview. When

Cont.

Case studies *Continued.*

coming for interview, it always amazes me how few people actually know that much about the company. Preparing shows the interviewer that you a) really want to work for that company (and won't start the job and find actually it's not for you and resign soon after) b) are pro-active (a crucial skill) and c) are not afraid of doing a bit more work than everyone else (again something which will no doubt be a question in most interviewers' minds).

Boden usually advertise buying vacancies. When drafting interview shortlists from CVs, they look for computer skills and numeracy. Interviewers aim to ascertain how well applicants work in a team, how they deal with problems or difficult situations, and also ask them questions specific to the company, such as what they know about Boden. Interviewees for buying jobs may be asked where they shop for clothes, who they think the potential customer is, and which companies are direct competitors, to establish whether they would fit into the Boden environment. It is not essential for applicants to have previous mail order experience, though some knowledge about how mail order differs from retail may be advantageous. The personnel department at Boden keeps CVs of applicants on file and buying managers play an active role in the recruitment of buying staff.

2. ASOS

Moriamo Oshodi is Head of Buying at the internet fashion retailer ASOS.com (see Figure 9.5). After studying A levels in Sociology, English Language and Literature and Theatre Studies she gained a BSc (Hons) Business Studies degree, before embarking on her buying career six years ago in House of Fraser's contemporary living department. She has also worked part-time in various fashion stores, including Ted Baker.

Role and responsibilities

Moriamo sums up her main responsibilities and tasks within the job as:

- setting the strategy for the womenswear department with the buyers (see Figure 9.6) and merchandise manager
- defining where growth can be achieved in the coming season
- planning product mixes within the departments
- working with the designer to agree the trend direction for the season
- development meetings with buyers to decide product direction
- participating in range review sign-offs with the retail director and buyer
- reviewing the past season's trading
- strategy meetings with key suppliers.

Figure 9.5 Moriamo Oshodi. Courtesy of ASOS.

Cont.

Case studies *Continued.*

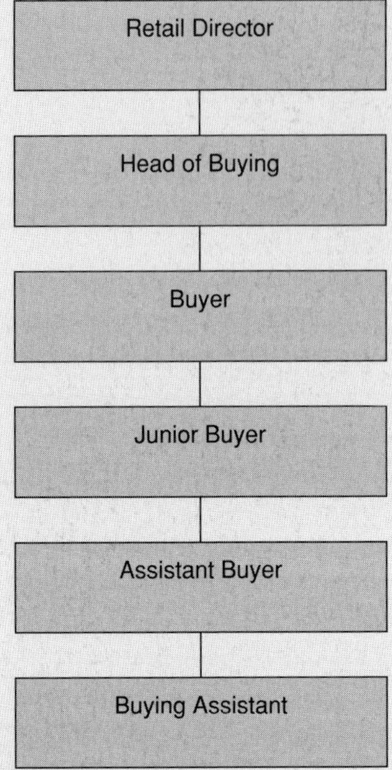

Figure 9.6 Structure of the buying department at ASOS.

Moriamo liaises with the press office to select merchandise for press releases and to advise which products from the range to push for PR. She regularly works with the company's creative team to select products for advertising campaigns and newsletters to their customers, and she explains here why this is an important part of her job:

> As an online-only company the presentation of our products is key. Therefore I work with our creative team to help produce twice-weekly email newsletters for womenswear and menswear which are sent to our database alerting customers to new products, trends and brands. I help produce styling guidelines for the photography team – as a company we shoot up to 100 products a day, three times a week.

She also collaborates with the creative team to produce ASOS, the company's monthly glossy fashion magazine which, she says, 'showcases ASOS.com own label and branded product in beautifully shot fashion stories as well as providing information on catwalk trends, celebrity style tips and fashion advice'. Her favourite part of the job is travelling, especially for product development and inspiration trips. She also enjoys managing the product development process and working with buyers to create the product ranges. In contrast, she says she finds the most difficult aspect to be 'ensuring that you maintain an overview of the whole business as well as your specific departments when you are absorbed in day to day business, but it is essential that you do this to ensure a strategic viewpoint'. Moriamo's performance at work is assessed on the basis of key performance indicators (KPIs), year-on-year growth of product sales and achieving the company's target margin. ASOS offers training courses for its buyers in subjects such as negotiation skills and management skills.

She lists the main factors which help buyers in the company to decide which garments to buy for their ranges as:

- customer profile
- trends
- past sales performance
- information from suppliers about products they are developing.

In order to monitor the competition within the womenswear market, Moriamo goes on weekly trips to review products in competing retailers' stores and does a monthly comparative shop to review competitors' prices.

Career advice

Moriamo's advice to anyone considering a career in buying is: 'hard work is the key to success – always persevere and put in the extra effort and it gains results. There is a lot of competition within the industry so dedication and a love of the job are essential'.

Chapter 10

Buying Branded Fashion Merchandise

This chapter concentrates on buying for stores that sell mainly branded fashion merchandise. Although some of these stores develop their own products, the emphasis of the buying role is on selecting finalised styles which have already been designed by other companies. The products are therefore sold with branded names rather than under the shop's own label. Most of these stores are independent companies which do not belong to large retail parent companies, and have a small number of outlets, from one to approximately 20 branches. Browns in London and Pollyanna in Barnsley are amongst the most well-known stores in the UK selling branded fashion merchandise. Most department stores develop their own ranges as well as buying branded fashion merchandise, with different buying teams working on separate ranges. Department stores may sell several fashion brands alongside each other or as individual concessions (see Chapter 8). John Lewis dropped its 'Jonelle' label in 2003 and now uses the store's name within its own products. In contrast, Debenhams sells various own labels under different names, aimed at different types of target customer, including 'J. Taylor', 'Casual Club' and 'Red Herring', disguising the fact that they are developed in-house exclusively for the department store chain.

The owners of independent stores often undertake the buying role along with numerous other tasks. They rarely employ merchandisers so this becomes the buyer's responsibility. Larger independent stores employ specialist buyers who usually have a background in retail management. Several retail chains selling branded fashion merchandise have expanded the number of their outlets during the last decade, including Envy (a division of the Alexon Group) USC and Republic, each with more than 50 stores in the UK, reflecting growing consumer demand for branded products.

There is less need in this type of job for qualifications or experience in fashion design than there is in a buying position for a chain store, since there is unlikely to be any design or product development involved in the role. It is more important that the buyer is familiar with the store's customers and their requirements, and it is much easier in this type of store for the buyer to gain a first-hand view of the clientele. The buying job for an independent store may be combined with a sales role within the shop particularly if there is only one outlet, as the buying position may not warrant a full-time salary. Buying

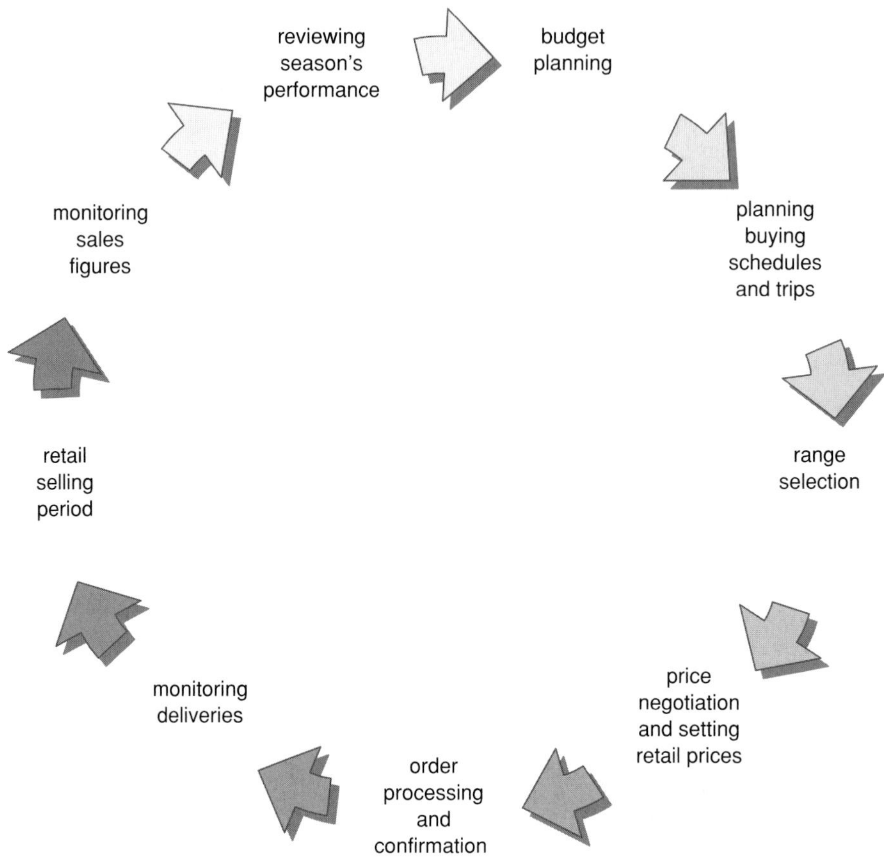

Figure 10.1 The buying cycle for branded fashion merchandise (Goworek 2006: 96).

fashion products for an independent store is different from buying non-fashion merchandise (see Figure 10.1) as it is essential that the buyer is able to select the right merchandise for the season and sell garments within a precise time-frame; the ability to gauge the right product at the right time is even more important in this field.

Budget planning and ordering merchandise

The buying role for branded merchandise often involves budget planning for future seasons whilst monitoring the budget for the current season. The buyer needs to predict how much money should be spent on a season's merchandise, and factors into the equation how much was sold last season, the constraints of space within the store (and therefore the number of garments which can be accommodated) and the amount of money which the company has available to spend. In effect, the buying cycle both starts and ends with a review of the previous season's performance, for an established store selling branded ranges, with each stage of the cycle providing information for the next step.

Most merchandise is ordered well in advance but the buyer needs to retain a certain portion of money to buy goods within the season itself – this is known as 'open-to-buy'. With this money, which could be in the region of 20% or more of the whole season's budget for a fashion-orientated store, the buyer has a safety net in case a key trend is missing from the range or if there is an opportunity to buy goods at a discounted price. Most of the merchandise bought from the open-to-buy budget is usually purchased from the supplier's existing stock, i.e. products which have already been manufactured and can be delivered almost immediately. Occasionally stock merchandise can be bought at a special reduced price, often referred to as 'off-price', particularly towards the end of a season, as the brand needs to sell it quickly to recover its costs before it is out of date. Mid-season trade fairs, aimed mostly at the home market, are held in several countries. These benefit buyers who have sold the season's range well and need some replacement styles, and buyers of branded labels who wish to sell ranges more frequently than twice per year. When planning budgets buyers need to take account of the fact that not all of the merchandise will be sold at full price and some garments will inevitably be marked down at the end of the season, thereby reducing the profits on some styles.

Selecting ranges of branded fashion merchandise

Buyers for independent stores usually visit showrooms to view ranges of branded fashion merchandise. Some buyers travel abroad to do this, typically visiting cities like Milan, Paris and London, where many fashion brands show at trade fairs and have showrooms. Trade fairs such as the *Pitti Uomo* menswear show in Florence have the advantage of exhibiting a wide selection of brands in the same place, allowing buyers to see many ranges within a short period, and identifying potential new brands to stock. Some buyers of branded merchandise may visit international fabric trade fairs, even though they are not involved in fabric selection, as they offer an early preview of forthcoming fabric and colour trends up to six months ahead of the buying period for the season (see Chapter 6). Buyers from many independent stores are likely to visit the same locations during peak buying periods, offering them an opportunity to network. As most such stores are not in direct competition with each other, being based in different towns and cities, a camaraderie may be built up between buyers from different shops, who often discuss the performance of brands.

An invaluable source of information about fashion brands is the 'Indicator' section of *Drapers* which contains regular surveys of 50 independent stores nationwide, from which charts are compiled of bestselling fashion brands in various market sectors. In one such survey in January 2006 *Drapers* reported that skinny jeans were the bestselling style for young women's fashion and the top five brands for the previous week in this sector were:

(1) Miss Sixty
(2) Firetrap
(3) Diesel
(4) Replay
(5) Fornarina.

This insight into the popularity of brands would be particularly useful for anyone launching an independent store stocking women's jeans, when considered in the context of the age range and lifestyle of the potential customer and depending on the selection of brands sold by competing stores locally.

Certain brands, especially the higher priced designer ready-to-wear labels, present their ranges at runway shows, to which buyers who are current or potential customers may be invited. Although catwalk shows were originally created as a method of showing new garment ranges to buyers they are now targeted primarily at the media with the press and celebrities taking priority over buyers in the seating arrangements. This situation should be welcomed by buyers as increased press coverage can mean higher sales for stockists of the brand. Some of the most prestigious brands are extremely selective about stockists for their products, only selling to those who meet their own strict criteria. This is the reverse of the usual situation for the buyer who is used to having the upper hand when selecting which brands to stock. Those who are fortunate enough to be accepted by the major brands can find that profit margins and sales are surprisingly low for these labels. However, it is worth stocking them to tempt in extra customers who are attracted by the prestige of famous names, even though they are more likely to purchase lower-priced merchandise. At the opposite end of the spectrum, brands which are known more through word-of-mouth than advertising or catwalk shows can enhance the image of the store. The buyer needs to have a thorough knowledge of the customer's lifestyle and culture to be able to spot such brands. The following list includes examples of fashion brands, classified by product and customer type:

- surf/skatewear brands for the younger menswear and womenswear market: Mambo, O'Neill, Quiksilver
- contemporary casual menswear and womenswear: Boxfresh, Diesel, Firetrap
- upper middle market womenswear brands: Libra, Olsen, Gerry Weber.

Buyers for independent stores need to review on a seasonal basis which brands should be stocked to offer a mix of labels to appeal to the store's customer base. This decision is based largely on sales figures which must be taken within the context of other factors such as reliability and service from the brand, weather conditions and brand awareness. A brand which has performed poorly in its first season in a store should not necessarily be discarded as the buyer may need to review the selling prices or may have confidence in the label being the next big thing. The buyer should be aware of the amount of promotion undertaken by the brand as this could have a significant impact on sales, particularly if a specific garment is due to be featured in an advertising campaign and is likely to be requested by customers. Independent fashion stores tend to target the middle to higher price bracket where the kudos created by the label can be as important as the styling features of the garment.

Retail price setting for branded merchandise

Branded fashion suppliers set cost prices for the garments within their ranges. These may be negotiable depending on the total volume of merchandise that the retail customer is buying, how long the store has been a stockist of the range, and the time of year (as brands may be keen to clear out stock at the end of a season). The buyer is responsible for setting retail prices, which are usually two to three times the cost price from the manufacturer in this sector of the market (a lower mark-up, on average, than the larger high street chains). Steve Cochrane, owner of Psyche in Middlesbrough, explains why the price of a garment and the brand's marketing strategy are very important factors to take into account when he makes buying decisions:

> In the High Street, they make things to a price, so if they want a T-shirt at £11.99, designers come up with some ideas, and they amend the style by saying: 'Lose that and that'. Everything on the high street to me is made down to a price, whereas branded is made up to an image, so that's the difference. We know our threshold prices. We know it's difficult to get over £100 for a pair of trousers and we know that £60 is a high volume price for us. If we found a pair of trousers that were £20, were reasonably made and we thought we could get £60 for them, we'd be very happy. Branding isn't as important on bottoms as it is on tops. It's a case of looking at the finish, looking at the fabric, when do they deliver and have they got any marketing? We ask them lots of questions. Some brands only deliver 50% of the merchandise we've ordered, and the contracts are weighted in their favour. We ask if it's good value, and how much they'll spend on marketing and where. This is one of the main criteria when we choose to stock a brand. Sometimes they do co-operative marketing with us, by listing us as one of their stockists, or if we took space in a local periodical they could share the costs with us. Some of them will do in-store merchandising or staff-training. Hugo Boss are by far the best at that. They're very successful and they deserve to be.

The buyer aims to have a target mark-up (or margin) throughout the range, but this is calculated as an average, allowing the buyer the flexibility to make a higher percentage of profit on some styles and less on others, where appropriate. The mark-up on the range needs to cover all of the overheads of running the store/s including such factors as rent, utility bills, wages, advertising and promotion, whilst retaining a profit for the owners or shareholders.

Cashflow can often be a problem for smaller fashion retailers, particularly when launching a first store. Payment for the merchandise has to be made shortly after delivery from the supplier but the store will not generate income until some time later during the subsequent weeks or months when customers begin to purchase the garments. For this reason an independent store may need to include loan payments as an overhead to help finance the business, and a new store would be unlikely to make a profit for at least the first year.

Processing orders and monitoring deliveries

Having seen the new season's range several months before delivery, buyers order garments either in the showroom or from their own offices. Waiting a few days to finalise orders is wise as this gives the buyer a chance to see several ranges and to make decisions which are more appropriate than those made during a showroom visit. The buyer then has an opportunity to discuss garments with sales staff, who may be able to offer a more commercial perspective.

Most independent retailers have their own system of paperwork to complete when ordering products (see Figure 10.2). The order sheets are submitted to the salespeople at the brand's office, detailing the style reference, colour, fabric, number of pieces, size ratio and expected delivery date. A buyer for an independent store buys smaller volumes than most department stores and needs to decide how many garments should be bought per size, as there is unlikely to be equal demand in each size. In a large chain store, the merchandiser usually takes responsibility for this but, for a smaller independent store it is part of the buyer's role.

For a store ordering ten garments per style the following size ratio could be specified by the buyer:

Size:	8	10	12	14	16	18
Quantity:	1	1	2	3	2	1

The quantities in a size ratio can be expressed either as numbers or percentages. The ratio selected for the order depends on previous sales history and how appropriate the style is considered to be for larger sizes. Typically, a short, fitted style may only be purchased in smaller sizes, but buyers could potentially increase sales by reconsidering stereotypes. Size 18 customers might actually be keen to buy such a style, since other retailers may be reluctant to take the risk of stocking it. Independent retailers need to regularly review their size ranges which may alter gradually each year. Selecting the right range of sizes is a crucial decision as sales will obviously be lost if there are insufficient garments in a particular size, leaving disappointed customers with a negative impression of the store.

This system is referred to as forward ordering, as garments are usually delivered several weeks or months after the order date. Manufacture of the garments often does not begin until initial orders have been made by customers, enabling the branded company to anticipate the quantity per style to be produced. However orders are not always on schedule and are sometimes incomplete. It

www.psyche.co.uk

Company

Season

Date

Department

Women ☐

Today's Exchange Rate

£1 =

Psyche Ltd. Buyer

Company rep.

Tel:

Delivery dates

ORDER No.

0051

201-203 + 215
Linthorpe Road
MIDDLESBROUGH
TS1 4AU
Tel: 01642 888333
Fax: 01642 221057

Women's Clothing Purchase Order

PSYCHE®

Style Name/No.	Fabric content	Colour	Size Scale													TOTAL	Description	Cost (Ex VAT)	Retail Price
			E			6	8	10	12	14	16	18							
			F	2	3	3H	4	4H	5	5H	6	6H	7	7H	8				
			G				XS	S	M	L	EL								
			H		24	26	27	28	29	30	31	32	33	34					
			J					ONE											

Figure 10.2 Psyche order sheet. Courtesy of Psyche.

is advisable to anticipate that some garments will arrive later than requested and the buyer will inevitably need to chase up progress on delivery with some suppliers. To pre-empt problems, the buyer might request an earlier delivery date than necessary, if the store has sufficient storage space. Another contingency plan could be to order slightly more stock than required from the more reliable companies, though the buyer needs to be confident that this merchandise can be sold profitably. When the garments arrive, the buyer completes the relevant paperwork to log delivery and compares this with the order sheets, to check that the merchandise is correct.

Monitoring sales figures and reviewing the season's performance

The buyer is likely to meet regularly with the store manager to gain feedback on sales figures and anecdotal information from customers. If a style is not selling well the sales staff may be able to tell the buyer some of the comments that customers have made about it. This is a distinct advantage of buying for an independent store as feedback is immediate and detailed, allowing the buyer to understand any problems with garments and respond quickly to customer feedback. Equally the buyer also needs to be prepared to accept that if a mistake has been made in selecting a garment for the range, he or she will know about it very quickly.

Weekly reports on sales figures are usually compiled by sales staff and can even be made available on a daily basis, allowing the buyer to review the range's performance constantly. The buyer can then decide whether to act by ordering extra merchandise to replace styles that are selling quickly or reduce the price of garments which are moving too slowly. Visual merchandising (VM) within the store and its windows can have a positive effect on sales figures for the styles chosen to be displayed. In an independent store the owner/buyer may also be responsible for VM, so is therefore able to anticipate the impact of the layout of the merchandise and amend it when required, in response to sales figures.

Buyers predict the amount of sell-through required of the range within a season, which means the amount of stock sold at full price prior to sale markdowns. The average target for the amount of each style selling at full price is likely to be around 75%. Pre-sale sell-through can be predicted separately for each brand stocked within the store as the buyer might expect certain brands to have stronger sales figures than others, depending on the customer's taste and lifestyle.

Repeat orders and markdowns

Stores often work to a target of 10 or 12 weeks' cover, meaning that they aim to sell out of a garment style within this period. If 10 pieces of a style have been bought but only one has been sold within four weeks, the buyer would estimate this garment to take another 36 weeks to sell out (nine garments selling at the rate of one every four weeks) which is obviously such a long time that it would still be on sale in the next season. Action therefore needs to be taken and the buyer would probably aim to mark it down early in the season to recoup as much money as possible rather than waiting to reduce it even further in the sale. This decision needs to be taken in the light of many other factors including the weather, which obviously has a major and often unpredictable effect on sales figures. A buyer might expect sales of swimwear to start slowly in the spring season but be prepared to wait for the weather to improve before considering a price reduction. Some independent retailers offer financial incentives such as bonuses to buyers to encourage them to make commercially sound decisions.

PR and promotion

The buyer for an independent store invariably has a wider role than a chainstore buyer and this can often extend to public relations (PR) and promotion for the company. Many independent fashion retailers advertise in the local press, particularly during sale periods. Some independents keep a database of customers' names and addresses and send a direct mailshot such as a postcard or invitation at key times of the year often offering discounts during a certain period. This can boost customer loyalty and help build up more of a relationship between the store and customers. As the customers have voluntarily left their personal details this can result in a higher response than would be expected from an unsolicited mailshot.

Some independent stores organise fashion shows for their customers as a promotional exercise. They may be held in-store in the evening by invitation only, or at an alternative venue. This can increase customer loyalty particularly if clients have been personally invited and a discount is offered for orders placed at the event. Apart from benefiting the customer the discount may be useful to the store if the fashion show is held at the beginning of the season as it offers an insight into which styles are likely to sell well, allowing the buyer to plan orders effectively. Fashion shows can be too expensive for most independent retailers as they cost several thousands of pounds if professional models, choreographers, sound and lighting systems are used.

Summary

Buying branded fashion merchandise for independent retailers or department stores differs from buying for retail fashion multiples in that the buyer is not involved in product development. Buyers in this sector may also be involved in monitoring deliveries as well as having direct contact with store managers to receive feedback and guidance on sales figures. Profit margins on the retail selling prices of branded merchandise are usually lower than those of most high street retailers.

References and further reading

Drapers (2006) Young women's fashion indicator. *Drapers,* 21 January: 10.

Goworek, H. (2006) *Careers in Fashion and Textiles.* Blackwell Publishing, Oxford.

Townsend, A. (2003) John L update does away with Jonelle. *Independent on Sunday,* 7 December.

CASE STUDIES IN BUYING BRANDED FASHION MERCHANDISE

1. Flannels

Marisa Shutt is a Ladieswear Buyer for Flannels, an independent retailer of designer clothing. After taking A levels Marisa graduated with a BSc (Hons) in Psychology from Sheffield University. She gained work experience at a London fashion house and worked backstage at fashion shows during London Fashion Week. She worked for four years in fashion retail sales in Warehouse, Oasis and Karen Millen before working as a merchandising assistant for Bhs Worldwide in London for one year. She then worked as a store manager/buyer for two years for Aquaint, a privately-owned concept store based in Covent Garden which showcased new emerging designers, before starting her current role in 2003. Flannels has outlets in Manchester, Altrincham, Leeds, Nottingham, Cardiff, Liverpool and Birmingham (see Figure 10.3) and Marisa is based at their Manchester Head Office.

Role and responsibilities

On a typical workday Marisa deals with emails and calls from existing suppliers and enquiries from numerous prospective new suppliers. She also receives daily calls from stores regarding special orders for clients. On a weekly basis she is responsible for stock analysis, which comprises:

- booking in deliveries of merchandise
- comparing the products which have been ordered to those which have been delivered
- producing and analysing weekly sales figures
- compiling weekly stockholding figures per season and location
- maintaining the correct balance of stock per location per supplier
- identifying stock issues
- analysing previous seasons' stock analysis and movements

Figure 10.3 Womenswear department at Flannels store in Birmingham.

Case studies *Continued.*

- compiling detailed spreadsheets to analyse categories of merchandise, e.g. tailoring
- monitoring the new season's incoming stock to the warehouse
- monitoring stockholding in the warehouse utilising weekly reports to move stock to relevant locations
- looking at fast-selling lines for in-season re-orders.

The Flannels buying department has close links to every other department in the company and Marisa says 'the buyers are involved in every aspect of decision-making regarding the stock and maximising its life cycle to increase sales'. On the ladieswear team there is one other buyer in addition to Marisa and an assistant buyer. The buyers liaise with the merchandiser who monitors spending throughout the season and ensures that they work within their budget for the season. All analysis on stock is done in unison with the merchandiser and, where necessary, action plans are devised together to ensure the best possible solution. Buyers negotiate any discounts with the suppliers at the buying appointment; and are responsible for ensuring that the accounts department have the information specific to each supplier necessary to pay the invoices correctly. On a daily basis Marisa checks the deliveries that are to be booked in the warehouse to enable her to inform stores of incoming stock, as they may be waiting for a reorder, or have waiting lists for a particular must-have item. This also allows her to monitor any late deliveries and to authorise any discrepancies, for example if items are sent in the incorrect size or colour and require her intervention to facilitate their return to the supplier. The returns department deal with faulty stock returned by stores and assess whether the garments need to be sent back to the supplier for inspection and, if necessary, repair or credit.

Marisa usually works simultaneously on two season's ranges. In October she will typically be concluding the buying for the following spring/summer for most brands, whilst working with in-season reorders for the current autumn/winter range. In November she commences viewing the 'pre-fall' collections in Milan which will be the start of buying for the subsequent autumn/winter, for delivery in July. She contacts the respective suppliers for the brands sold within the store each season and requests biographical information on the brands and training manuals, if available. Store training is also arranged where suppliers visit each of the stores and talk to the staff about the ranges. Marisa monitors the current season's buying performance weekly through reports which assess each brand. At the end of each season, prior to the sale, all the information on each brand per store is collated and their relative success determines the respective budget allocated to that specific brand for the following season.

Marisa's responsibilities include managing the financial budgets for buying merchandise for Flannels stores each season. She allocates a budget per brand/per store based upon the overall seasonal budget dictated by the managing director. Budgets per supplier are increased or decreased according to season on season performance of the brand. She sets up new budget spreadsheets for ladieswear each season, updating them daily when orders are placed. She also monitors the actual amount of money spent on products weekly by the company and the profit margin made.

To select the range of garments sold by Flannels, Marisa attends buying appointments, making selections from the collections where appropriate. She travels to Milan, Paris and London for buying appointments and trade shows at least once a month, on trips lasting between one and ten days. The buyers also carry out comparative shops at least four times per year in these locations, visiting stores with a similar concept to Flannels where they assess the product ranges on offer, fixtures and merchandising within the store and customers. Marisa explains how she finds out about the company's potential customers and their opinions on the product range:

> I visit the stores at least once weekly, and talk to the stores managers daily to get their feedback. Out of the buying season I work on the shop floor serving the customers as much as possible. There is really no substitute for this because you are working with the product and understanding it from every angle, how it merchandises on the shop floor, its overall impact within the store, fit issues etc. We have our own local Manchester-based PR company who organise customer events and promotions to quantify more scientifically customer opinions and maximise exposure for new customers.

For each product she selects for Flannels, Marisa is required to check data regarding the style, to process and send the order, and to deal with the relevant administration. She continually assesses the orders which have been delivered and liaises with suppliers to chase outstanding stock and answer queries, mostly concerning cancellation, pricing or deliveries (e.g. incorrect styles or colours delivered or additional units delivered which have not been ordered). She places orders using a Microsoft Excel spreadsheet template. The supplier, season, mark-up and delivery dates are entered in the sheet heading, with the sizes ordered placed along the top of the spreadsheet. The following information is then recorded for each style:

- supplier's product code
- cost price and retail price
- style description (created by buyer inputting order)
- supplier's colour code and Flannels colour reference
- product type and category codes used at the bottom of the order for analysis.

Each of the Flannels stores has a branch number which is inputted onto the spreadsheet. An overall quantity is entered per style for each store, once the buyers are happy with the overall spend/selection for each store. Finally size ratios for each style are decided, proportionate to the sales of the previous season.

The total figures per size, colour and style are then entered for each branch. The spreadsheet has an automated calculation, which computes total order quantities by branch and per category, which can be compared to the original budgets. The bottom of this spreadsheet also shows the overall margin for that

Cont.

Case studies *Continued.*

particular order. Once the order is completed the supplier's copy is printed. A purchase order is obtained from stock control and this is sent to the supplier. It is important that all payment details for new suppliers and terms and conditions are sent with each order. Pro forma payments can sometimes be made, where full- or part-payment for goods ordered is paid prior to physically receiving the goods.

Marisa begins preparing for each seasonal sale three weeks in advance, then spends a further eight weeks working on it until the sale ends. This entails:

- compiling sale instruction packs for staff within stores
- marking down each item individually according to its performance during the season
- keying in markdowns on the computer system
- analysing the profit margin per season
- specifying further markdowns after the initial days of the sale
- writing instructions to stores to recall stock back to the warehouse after the sale whereupon it is assessed and either sent to the company's sale shop or reserved for clearance sales.

To sum up the most enjoyable and challenging aspects of her job, Marisa says:

> I enjoy being exposed to the creativity and innovation of fashion. The time, effort and dedication that it takes whole teams of people to create a collection are sometimes inspirational. I admire people really who believe in their work and in these cases it is a pleasure to buy their collections and make them a success. There are very few companies in the UK like Flannels where you can experience the freedom of buying for a privately-owned company. I buy for ladieswear, which means everything from mainline ready-to-wear collections through to sunglasses and shoes. In larger companies you tend to be a buyer for a particular category, but I'm privileged to be working with every aspect of ladieswear from head to toe. However, the buying season is becoming longer with fewer breaks because labels are presenting more collections, so you have to be prepared for the concept of working for long periods of time without a day off. This is sometimes difficult because although the opportunity to travel is a privilege you can face long periods of time away from home.

Skills and training

Marisa considers computer literacy to be essential for her job because she works with Microsoft Word and Excel constantly, and she has studied courses on Excel from introductory to advanced level. She also states that the ability to adapt to new computer systems is extremely useful and that numeracy is important (although a strong GCSE grade should be adequate, since buyers predominantly work with percentages). Here she describes some of the other skills required to work successfully in this type of buying role:

> Teamwork is essential in the buying department, as often deadlines for orders have to be met and workload can mount up quickly. Usually there are two buyers present at any appointment and often the day's orders will have to be split to meet deadlines. Likewise if an appointment is running behind schedule the pair buying may have to part ways to attend appointments alone. The role of the buyer's assistant is integral, whilst they are predominantly based at Head Office they are often required to fax or email information over to the buyers whilst they are out of the company. Also they often need a second opinion on issues at head office in the buyer's absence so a strong chain of communication is essential. Whether it is addressing issues in the instance of being physically absent from the situation and having to make yourself implicitly understood, or simply being proficient and honest with prospective suppliers on the phone, it's important to be comfortable and confident with your own opinions. Good organisational skills are key – planning the ongoing buying schedule means making appointments in good geographical proximity to each other and planning routes to destinations you may have never travelled to before. Often you need to be equipped with the information and ability to go to any appointment unplanned, as you may get some information about an emerging label when you are out on a buying trip and have to use the resources available to you to locate it and find out whom to buy it from.

Career advice

Marisa's advice to someone considering running their own independent clothing store would be:

> There is no substitute for shop floor experience. Despite my degree in psychology I was a strong candidate for my current role due to my continuous shop floor experience. Really consider the concept that you would like to create within your store. It is important to have an angle, there are many stockists of popular brands within the UK; stores that become a success are those with their own identity. For the customer the reason to visit that particular store above all others is for the unique experience it provides them.

2. Tin Fish

Pete Mellor is the owner of 'Tin Fish', a footwear retailer with two outlets in Leicester (see Figure 10.4). He is responsible for managing the company, which he started 15 years ago, and buying the footwear range. Pete studied BSc (Hons) Maths and Management at Manchester University for two years before leaving to work in various jobs including insurance underwriting and sales management for a car dealership.

Launching a footwear retail outlet

In 1991 Pete decided to go self-employed and considered importing classic cars, but when the market for them imploded he had to evaluate other options, as he explains:

> Some friends of mine studied footwear design at Leicester and I'd been to some local factories with them, so I thought 'what about shoes?' We started in Silver Arcade in Leicester, which was full of quirky independents selling mainly vintage clothing at the time, but no-one was selling shoes there. My friend was thinking about opening a clothes shop there and I couldn't believe how cheap the rent was. I worked it out and realised I wouldn't need to sell all that much to set up a shop there.

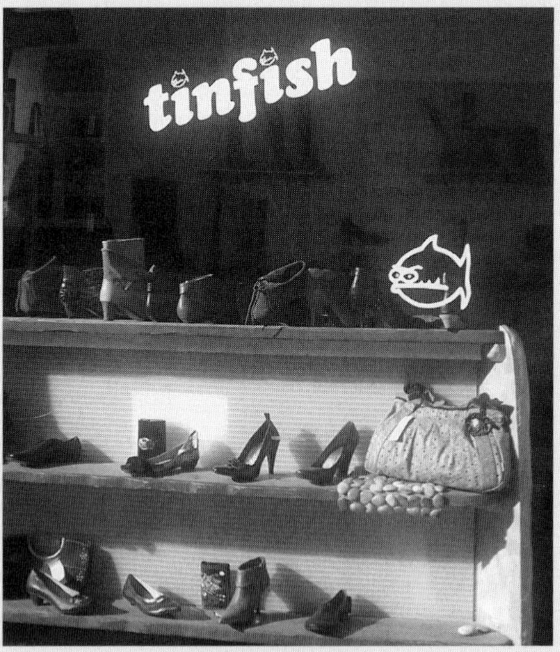

Figure 10.4 Tin Fish store, Stoneygate, Leicester.

With a friend in the shoe trade and a potential site, Pete says he was sure if he put his mind to it he couldn't fail. He rented a shop for £40 a week with the first month rent free. It had been a storeroom, so he used the first month to decorate it, varnish the floorboards and fit it out with metal tables made from train scrap by his flatmate who was a sculptor. He chose 'fish' to be part of the shop's name because his star sign is Pisces and he remembered learning at school that the term Tin Fish was used to describe torpedoes. He describes the processes he went through to launch the shop in 1991:

> There were still a lot of shoe factories in Leicester and Northampton at the time, which were struggling, otherwise I think they wouldn't have had time to deal with me. My friend and I narrowed it down to about 12 factories who were making shoes for Schuh, Office and bigger companies, and we spent the next two weeks driving round meeting the sales managers. I'd say to them I was looking for fashion styles similar to the 'Red or Dead' brand. I had to buy anything, to a point, including samples, and the car sales experience came in handy for negotiating. Although it seems completely irrelevant it gave me a real grounding for dealing with and selling to people at different levels. Learning to overcome objections was useful. I got introduced to Wayne Hemingway at a trade show in London when he ran Red or Dead and he was helpful and keen to sell to us, because we were one of the few shops outside London buying his range. We sold a lot of their shoes and I drove to their offices every week to choose stock from their shelves, putting them in the shop the next day. There was no forward buying in the first year. On the day we opened we had 25 styles. We sold a lot to students and that sort of market, and it worked. I don't think you could start off the same way today. To set up your own store now, you'd have to go to trade fairs to make all the contacts. Ninety-five per cent of shoes in my shops now are made abroad, whereas when I started it was 100% UK products. One of the few companies I know that has survived is a Northamptonshire factory called George Cox, which was one of the first suppliers I dealt with, selling classic riding boots and now beetle-crushers and winklepickers.

Role and responsibilities

Pete's role varies according to the time of year. From March to May and August to December he is involved in selecting footwear for the store. During August he starts to look at products for the following spring/summer season. The main responsibilities of his job include:

- meeting representatives from footwear brands
- attending footwear trade fairs
- comparative shopping to assess competing retailers' ranges
- organising seasonal sales
- paperwork (opening post, receiving invoices, checking deliveries and writing cheques)
- liaising with store managers and sales staff
- organising promotional activities for the company.

Cont.

Case studies *Continued.*

Pete describes the work he is involved in throughout the year:

On a typical day I'll have one, maybe two appointments with either reps or agents coming in here to show me footwear ranges or I go and visit them, usually in London or sometimes in the Midlands, as there still seem to be a lot of shoe trade people based around Leicestershire. The morning's taken up with phonecalls and post really, then checking emails. I've got a manager for each store and I delegate to them so I don't have to get involved with the real nitty-gritty. Two or three times a week I check on what orders we've got outstanding, what's due to come in, what's late and how to action that: if it's too late I decide whether to cancel it, or ask for discount from the supplier.

When we're not buying it's a question of organising sales, usually in high summer and just after Christmas. We have a flat period in January/February and then June/July when we're not doing any buying. As this summer's worked out (2006) we've had such a fantastic sale we've had to buy products especially for it. We only do this every now and again when we get a style that sells because it's reduced. The style was right, but the price was wrong. When we reduce prices we do it quite substantially, anywhere up to 60% or sometimes more. Sometimes we'll buy more of that style in cheaply because there'll be some stock available from the supplier. Generally I try to sell what we've already got, because sale time is a chance to clear the decks and make room for new stock. We always start our summer sales relatively late compared to other stores, about mid July, which can cause frustration for customers in the first two weeks of July who ask when the sale is on.

Pete employs a manager for his city centre store who assists with some of the buying decisions, particularly setting retail prices. She provides him with a link to the staff and organises the practicalities of running the store, ensuring shelves are clean and shoes are out and priced, as well as assessing sales figures. As Tin Fish is a small company there are no set meetings. Pete explains how his manager can provide him with useful information from the shopfloor, influencing the way he purchases products:

I might be on the computer and look at the figures and think 'that style's not gone particularly well' and she could say 'but a lot of people asked for it' or if it's early in the season we might have had a lot of people trying it on, saying 'I'm going to come back for that later'. If the sizing was too big, for example, we might have sold out of all of the small sizes. So I could look on the computer and see that we've got lots of 6s, 7s and 8s left which we've had in for weeks. She might say 'if you got some more 3s, 4s and 5s in you would sell more', which is not always clear just from looking at the figures.

As with most fashion retailers, one of the major factors that influences sales volume for Tin Fish is the weather. Pete describes how it affects his buying strategy:

The weather is such a key thing and it's changed: the summer usually starts at the end of May and then goes on until October. The vast majority of our sandals don't get looked at until early May, certainly after Easter. When you look at sales for Birkenstock, which is a classic one-strap, every year we sell none in March, maybe two in April, one or two at the end and beginning of May, then in June/July sales of them go crazy, in August/September it starts to dip, then in October it finally dies. We always seem to have good weather in September and early October, so the summer seems to have shifted to later in the year. The long range weather forecasts are interesting but can still be wrong. We heard about the worst ever winter coming in 2005 and it never really happened. The spring/summer 2006 season was strange because we had such a poor start in April and May when the weather was so bad. Then from 1st June it just seemed to pick up, the sun came out and sales were phenomenal.

The big companies like Schuh, Faith and Office are chasing suppliers for spring stock in January and it's not working, so they're reducing it but we're not getting ours until February/March. In big companies merchandisers look at sales figures on computers and if it's not selling they think 'get rid of it'. It's harder for them to have their eyes on the shop floor. You would probably only sell spring product that early to the odd one or two fashionistas, rather than the vast majority of customers. It's the same with boots for autumn/winter. Other shops stock them in July, but boots don't sell until October, which suppliers admit, but the big stores are pressurising the suppliers to get them in – it's a competitive thing. The last couple of years we've used an Excel computer program to analyse figures en masse which helps you realise when you start selling certain types of shoe rather than brands. We can stagger deliveries more so we can get a slightly more efficient sell-through.

Pete travels to the international footwear trade fairs GDS in Dusseldorf for mainstream styles and 'Micam' in Milan for more fashion-led brands. He recently ventured into developing own label Tin Fish footwear. Though factories normally require minimum order quantities which are too large for small retailers, a contact recommended a factory supplying small orders of less than 20 pairs. Pete explains the advantages and disadvantages of launching an own label range:

Though the vast majority of the factory's styles were inappropriate, we sifted through and changed things slightly, getting rid of some of the over-the-top detailing. We didn't design them from the ground up, but we had some input and the profit margin was good. We got them delivered in September and started selling them in October. We had such a good reaction we thought we could order more before Christmas, but couldn't get them delivered until Christmas day because of the shipping lead times from China. We looked at air freighting them to speed it up and although this made the margin lower we knew we could sell them, so we got them in, because after Christmas things become less desirable. The problem with the second batch was that the quality was poor and we got returns. That's when you feel it as an independent, because the cost of sending them all back to China is so expensive. We haven't bought from them again.

Cont.

Case studies *Continued.*

When asked which aspects of his job he enjoys most, Pete's response is:

> Independence, being my own boss, having nobody to answer to, the people I've met over the years, suppliers who've become friends, and I enjoy the banter. The most difficult thing is getting it right and predicting. The hardest part now is what not to buy. Because we've been around a few years, we've got a good reputation and we pay our bills, so we get a lot of phonecalls, and agents who I've worked with over the years who have changed brands ring me. Before you know it you've looked at 40 ranges and you're only halfway through the season. Deciding who to drop when you introduce a new brand is the hardest bit.

Pete assesses the company's sales figures on a six-monthly basis, from February to July and August to January, breaking them down by brand. He analyses how much money they've made (apart from during the seasonal sale) to give him benchmark figures, then looks at the performance of individual ranges (around 30 in total), highlighting the top and bottom five or six. He decides on a cut-off sales figure, below which he seriously reduces orders from a brand. Conversely, he aims to buy more from brands where he identifies a good sell-through rate. If a brand performs badly for two consecutive seasons, taking into account winter and summer, he stops buying it.

Tin Fish sell roughly 230–240 women's styles and 120–140 men's styles at any one time. A file is kept for every brand with individual sales figures per style in every colour. Before each buying meeting with a supplier Pete looks at that brand's file and analyses the figures. He finds that seasonal sales can skew the figures, making some brands seem better sellers than they are, so he analyses each brand at full retail selling prices, in terms of numbers sold and profitability. He works on an average markup of 51% profit. Here he describes the factors which help him to decide which products to buy:

> Sometimes I'll just get it out of the bag and I'll go 'yes' straight away. A brand that sums up our female customer is Camper because it's quite quirky, very wearable and comfortable. I think we're seen as more of a comfort-orientated, casual store than a high fashion, glamorous, high-heeled shop. Camper will take a basic shape which is quite wearable and fits most people and they'll put some really interesting little design detail there, so I find it relatively easy to buy. There are certain shoes within a range that just stand out as being right for Tin Fish. So there are brands that I rely on for our typical look: Fly, Camper, Bronx and Diesel, which are pretty much our bestsellers. We can usually say whether a style looks right for a particular customer who buys a lot from us. You can't rely on just one person, but she typifies the type of customer that we get. Equally we know we need a slightly younger product for newer customers. There are also some generic styles we buy, so every brand will do a sandal, and we need to find the one that's best-suited. You can buy a basic toe-post flip-flop anywhere, but it's got to be interesting and reasonably priced.
>
> I used to spend more time in the shop three or four years ago but now I look at sales figures and get feedback about customers more from the staff and

managers. Sometimes when I'm doing the buying if I like a particular product and the girls in the shop (who are mostly students) agree, the chances are it's going to be a good one. The odd one or two shoes I definitely know to buy, but the rest of it is a lot more difficult. That'll be down to other staff, what's in the fashion press and certain key looks. If you go to Micam or GDS you'll see a certain theme coming through. If it's on everyone's stand it's going to translate onto the high street, so it's useful to go to those shows.

As Tin Fish is a small retailer Pete is involved in all aspects of promotion for the company:

We advertise in 69 magazine which is a high quality glossy giveaway, covering the whole Midlands. We hand out flyers, mainly in customers' bags and every now and then we'll get someone to wander round town handing them out. We've also used buses and local papers for advertising. We recently started a loyalty card where we gave customers £20 if they bought three pairs of shoes, which gave us a useful database of customers. We've just started a website so we have different avenues to try and retain customers. It seemed to be the right way to go, seeing the students and new generation coming through who are so internet-savvy, buying online and socialising through computers. It's more of a viewing site, an introduction to the shops and we've got a lot of enquiries from it with quite good feedback. There are just a few shoes on there at the moment to see how it goes and to iron out the faults. We've got someone who can maintain the site for us and put the shoes on as soon as they come in, so it can be more of a reflection of the store today, to open us up to a much bigger audience.

Pete's advice to anyone considering running their own independent clothing or footwear store is:

Start off small. Keep your overheads down. Try and find a cheap unit, have a concession or start off within somebody else's store maybe. Too many people launch into a decent-sized shop paying a ridiculous rent and in six months' time they're gone. In the first two years I thought we were getting nowhere and we weren't making much money. It's great when you pick a winner and it turns out to be one of your bestsellers, then it validates what you're doing. Equally what you think is a winner can turn out to be an absolute duffer and it challenges you and makes you think. I keep myself in check because it's easy to have a good season and get carried away. We had a reality check this year because we had such a terrible start to the season. Each season you learn more, which you don't always realise until you look back on it, and I'm still learning.

Chapter 11

Fashion Marketing for Buyers

The purpose of marketing is to maximise a company's sales by selling products which meet consumers' needs effectively. Easey states that: 'a central component of the definition of fashion marketing is satisfying customers' needs profitably' (2002: 44). Marketing is not confined solely to promotional strategies, but can be applied to a wide variety of activities within a company, including the product development process in which the buyer plays an important part. This chapter explains those aspects of marketing in which the fashion buyer is regularly involved. When selecting a fashion range, the buyer has to constantly consider the customer's needs in relation to the product, in order to make the range a commercial success. The market for a fashion product comprises all of the potential buyers and sellers of the product, i.e. customers and retailers. It is an integral part of the fashion buyer's role to be familiar with the type of customers at which the product is aimed, and to be aware of similar product ranges offered by competitors.

The fashion marketing mix

The marketing mix is the combination of variables that contribute to the ability of a brand or product to meet consumers' needs profitably, often referred to as the four Ps (see Figure 11.1). This model has also been expanded to five or seven Ps by various authors.

Every fashion brand has its own unique marketing mix, with each of the four Ps contributing to the customer's perception of the brand's image. Fashion buyers have a significant influence on the product and price elements of the marketing mix of fashion brands and products. The marketing mix for Marks and Spencer's clothing can be briefly summarised as follows:

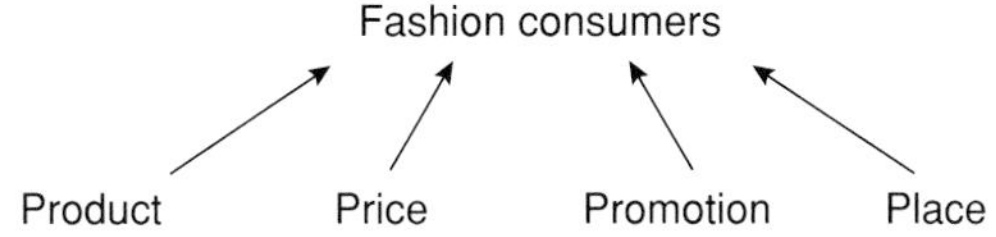

Figure 11.1 The fashion marketing mix.

- Product – menswear, womenswear and childrenswear, including outerwear and underwear ranges, with a reputation for good quality merchandise
- Price – middle mass market
- Promotion – word-of-mouth, press and TV advertising, in-store promotions
- Place – variety chain store with over 450 stores in the UK, based in town centres and retail parks, and numerous branches in over 30 other countries.

When a buyer selects the products to be sold by a fashion retailer, it is essential that decisions made in relation to the product reflect the perceived needs of the customer. Buyers have to resist the temptation to allow personal taste to intrude on such decisions, particularly if they are in a different age bracket from the store's potential customers. Buyers play an influential part in determining the selling price (and negotiating the cost price) of the product, and this also needs to be a customer-focused decision. The buyer's input to the promotion of the range is usually limited to the provision of press samples, unless the company operates as a small independent retailer, where the buyer may also be responsible for PR and advertising. 'Place' refers to the method of distribution of merchandise to the customer, which is largely through retail multiples or mail order for fashion products, as detailed in Chapters 8 and 9. The buyer's contact with the company's retail outlets is usually restricted to occasional visits to stores.

The fashion product life cycle

Fashion products have a limited life cycle, more so than most other products. The buyer needs to anticipate the expected life cycle of a fashion product in terms of the number of phases or seasons for which it is offered to customers. The product's life cycle may be extended by amending a style gradually from one season to the next, by offering new colourways or adding styling details. The product life cycle (see Figure 11.2) can be applied to a generic product type, or to a specific style stocked by a retailer. Jeans are probably the longest

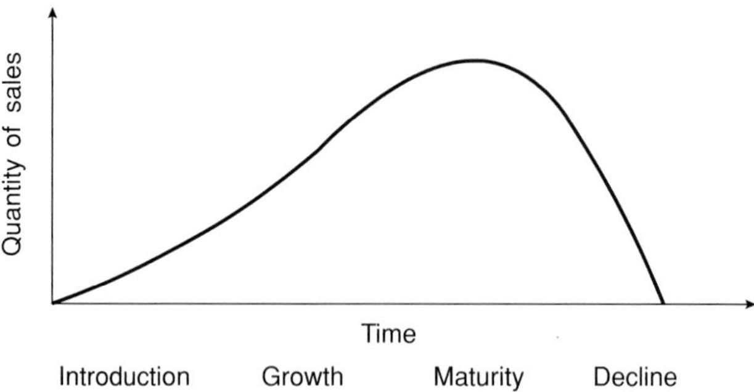

Figure 11.2 The product life cycle.

surviving example of a classic item, having been introduced in the nineteenth century, before entering the growth stage as a mainstream fashion item in the 1950s and are currently positioned in the maturity stage. Within the jeans market, boot-cut jeans are also in the maturity stage, having been re-introduced to the mass market in the mid 1990s, based on styling from the 1970s.

Even within such a classic product area there are fads, such as the short-term fashion for the hems of jeans to be decorated with feathers and beads, inspired by Gucci, in 1999. Fads evidently have a shorter product life cycle than classic styles and the buyer needs to predict the length of this timespan precisely to assist range planning. The product life cycle can last from four weeks up to several decades but for most women's fashion styles it is likely to last from six months to a year. Most menswear and childrenswear styles have a longer product life cycle than womenswear items though girlswear is responding increasingly quickly to mainstream trends. A concept closely linked to that of the product life cycle is opinion leadership, the theory that opinion leaders within society are the first to experiment with new styles before they are seen and later adopted by the mass market.

Introduction

Most new fashion styles are introduced at designer level. At this stage the product is obviously in a high price bracket and only available to a limited number of customers. The style may then be promoted through press coverage of runway shows which generates interest from fashion consumers. Buyers and designers identify products which are at the introduction stage of the product life cycle on directional shopping trips and through fashion forecasting information. Buyers working for stores which sell contemporary designer-level merchandise can rely mainly on instinct and experience to decide which styles to stock, as most of their products are at the introduction stage, and the minority are in the growth stage, of the product life cycle.

Growth

A limited number of the numerous fashion styles introduced in designer ready-to-wear ranges are adopted by the mass market. During the growth stage of the product life cycle, versions of these styles become available in the more fashion-conscious high street multiples. As designer ranges are shown on the catwalks almost six months ahead of a season this often gives the mass market the opportunity to introduce similar styles within the same season. The promotion of mass market fashion products within the fashion press usually peaks within the growth stage.

Maturity

In the maturity stage of the product life cycle a style is stocked by an increasing number of mass market stores and the maximum sales volume is achieved. At this stage the style may be diluted by conservative or lower price-bracket retailers, and variations may be introduced by fashion-led retailers. The maturity stage may be protracted for several years if the style becomes a classic item.

Decline

In the decline stage of the product life cycle a style is likely to be discounted to ensure that sales are made whilst it remains a wearable item for fashion consumers. A classic item may have a long decline stage. Since many fashion items from previous decades are subsequently revived, some styles may re-enter the introduction stage of the product life cycle within a relatively short period after decline.

Customer profiles

Most fashion retailers define the type of customer at whom their products are aimed, describing them as potential or target customers. The potential customers may not currently shop at the buyer's store but include the type of customer to whom the company aims to sell its products. Focusing on a particular area of the market in this way is referred to as market segmentation. It is usually the responsibility of a retailer's marketing department to specify customer profiles and give buyers and designers an overview of the type of consumer for whom the product ranges should cater. Customer profiles are usually brief written descriptions of potential customers but can also be compiled visually in the form of a collage. The key elements which can be contained in customer profiles include:

- demographic segmentation: factual information such as gender and age group
- psychographic segmentation (lifestyle): type of employment, family aspects, type of housing, typical holiday locations, likes and dislikes
- geographic segmentation: typical locations for customers, cities, towns, villages and type of housing.

A customer profile can be approached in various ways. Often it describes the typical customer, also known as the core customer, who shops at the specified retailer's stores. This could take the form of a description of an average customer who can sometimes be given a fictitious first name. Customer profiles can also be broader to incorporate several types of the retailer's customers. Some companies prefer to focus on the customer's aspirational lifestyle, rather than the life which most of them actually lead, as fashion very often reflects customers' aspirations. Fashion retailers have many customers in addition to the core customer who may be older or in a lower income bracket than the typical customer whom the buyer is targeting. Lifestyle is increasingly superseding age as the most important factor in product selection, and a retailer which aims at a core age range of 25–35 will probably find in practice that they have customers aged from 15 to 70. However it is still relevant to aim the range primarily at 25- to 35-year-olds, as this is likely to be the age bracket in which many of those younger and older customers perceive themselves.

It is important for retailers to review the life style and tastes of the potential customer regularly if they wish to maintain a particular age range. Maintaining a consistent group of customers can be a risk as the group's customer profile will age and they will become less likely to take an interest in fashion. This type of scenario may have contributed to the financial problems at Laura Ashley in recent years. Targeting an older market segment, such as the over 55s, can also be a profitable venture as many people in this bracket have reached the peak of their earnings, own their own homes and no longer have dependent children, resulting in a high disposable income which could be spent on clothing.

The income bracket of the customer can be less crucial than it first sounds, as it often does not correlate with the amount of money he or she is prepared to spend on clothes. High earners may not consider clothes to be a spending priority, perhaps because most of their time is devoted to work or they may have large financial commitments such as a mortgage. Conversely a low earner, particularly in the younger age group, may prioritise spending on clothes because of lack of long-term financial commitments and more time available for socialising and so have a relatively high disposable income. Buyers need to be familiar with customer profiles to ensure that they aim ranges at the relevant life style, considering where, when and why certain garments will be worn. If the retailer is targeting customers at management level this will probably be reflected by including formal office wear such as classic tailoring in the range, at a middle to high price bracket. A younger target customer in a lower income bracket, on the other hand, is likely to require clothing primarily for socialising, such as leisurewear and clubwear.

Marketing research methods

Some fashion retailers undertake market research to define their potential customers or to find consumer opinion on the product range. This may be done by the retailer's own marketing department or it may be carried out by an independent marketing research company. Research which is exclusive to one company and may involve contacting customers directly is referred to as primary research (or field research). Secondary research involves looking at information and data which have already been published (also called desk research). Despite its name secondary research usually happens first as it can be much quicker and more economical to seek existing information. However primary research is often the only appropriate method to use particularly when the aim is to find out the opinions of specific types of customer on certain products.

Primary research

Methods of primary research include:

- surveys by questionnaire, either face-to-face or by post
- focus groups
- interviews.

The focus group is a popular method for eliciting consumer opinions and involves the careful selection of a group of potential or actual customers who are asked a series of questions or given topics for discussion. This can result in in-depth information but must be regarded with caution as it is not necessarily representative of most customers, because of the small size of the sample. This can be overcome partly by planning several focus group sessions with different participants, possibly in different cities, to allow for geographic differences. With all market research it is important that the researcher aims to be unbiased (though this is never entirely possible) to gain realistic and useful consumer feedback. Researchers should not offer their own opinions or try to guide the participants to anticipated responses. Even stating the name of the retailer could influence customers favourably towards a range as participants often have a natural willingness to give the 'right' or expected answer. For this reason, it may be best to use an independent marketing research company.

The results of market research surveys are only as good as the questions which have been asked and the professionalism of the market research team. Though market research is generally the responsibility of the marketing department, buyers can initiate informal market research by gathering a group of the retailer's customers in a focus group to request opinions on a range which is currently being developed.

Store visits and comparative shopping

It is an integral part of most buyers' jobs to visit branches of their own retailers' stores and this can be categorised as primary research. Store visits involve speaking to salespeople who can give valuable feedback from constant direct contact with customers. This could enable a buyer to discover why a particular garment or range did not sell well, or conversely, the factors which contributed to the successful performance of a range. The best times to visit store branches are just before the development of a new range so that the buyer can learn from current successes and mistakes, or during a markdown promotion when the store is likely to be full of customers. Oasis sends members of buying teams from management to trainee level to stores for a day, to act anonymously as assistants in the changing rooms, which gives them first-hand experience of customers' responses to their ranges. Ideally a buyer should visit stores several times per season at different branches to become familiar with various types of customer.

'Mystery shoppers' are also used by some stores to gain anonymous feedback from customers which is fed back to the buying department. Some retailers also allow sales or design personnel from their garment suppliers to undertake store visits in their own branches. This offers them direct access to feedback on the ranges which they have designed and manufactured and influences the way in which they develop future ranges for the retailer. Comparative shopping trips were discussed in Chapter 3 and are essential for the buyer to gain knowledge of the products and services on offer to the customer within competing stores. Comparative shopping can be classed as an observational primary research method.

Secondary research

Sources of secondary research for fashion markets include:

- *Market Intelligence* (*Mintel*)
- *Retail Intelligence*
- Key Note
- government reports from the Office of Public Sector Information (OPSI, formerly HMSO)
- *Retail Directory – UK*
- annual company reports
- trade press: *Drapers, Lingerie Buyer.*

Mintel is published monthly and offers overviews of UK markets for specific products of many types including fashion markets such as womenswear retailing, footwear and lingerie. It includes information such as the estimated market value and the main competitors within the market. *Retail Intelligence* has a similar format, focusing exclusively on sectors of the retail market. UK government reports from the OPSI are published by the Stationery Office and can be purchased directly or found in libraries. There are several Stationery Office reports of relevance to fashion markets including *Regional Trends,* which details the average amount of disposable income available to a particular age group and the amount of money spent on average per capita on clothes in a particular region. This could influence a fashion retailer to decide on a particular area in which to open a new branch. Fashion trade magazines often feature articles about particular market sectors.

The *Retail Directory – UK* lists multiple and independent retailers of all types including fashion stores, with information such as the location of the head office, the number of outlets and annual turnover; a European edition is also available. This is very useful to retailers who wish to have more knowledge of their competitors, students who wish to apply for jobs and for manufacturers wishing to contact potential new customers. All public limited companies publish annual reports which are available to the general public either by requesting a copy from head office (usually free of charge) or via the company website. The annual report is largely financially based, containing a profit and loss account and balance sheet for the previous year, but it also summarises subsidiaries of the company and types of product with the intention of enticing potential shareholders to invest in the business. Fashion students will find most if not all of the above publications in university libraries.

Test-marketing fashion products

Certain retailers test-market fashion products by selling them in a limited number of branches in advance of the season. Only large retailers are able to do this because the quantity that would be produced for test marketing (perhaps 500 pieces of a style) can be equivalent to the amount for a total order in a smaller retailer. Test-marketing fashion products can be problematic as customers are influenced by contemporary styles and if they are shown garments ahead of the season they may not be able to anticipate what they will want to wear at that time. Test-marketing can be more useful when launching product concepts which are new to the store (such as an interiors range or nightwear) by trialling them in a representative sample of stores in the first season, minimising the expense and possible risk of introducing the concept to all stores immediately. Independent retailers can test-market products by inviting customers to fashion shows where samples of new styles are modelled and discounts offered for advance orders. Another form of test-marketing is to send preview mail order catalogues to a selected group of customers in order to predict demand for a new season's styles, offering discounts to encourage purchases (see Chapter 9).

Fashion consumer behaviour

The buyer should consider carefully the factors which persuade consumers to purchase fashion products. When buying, customers seek to meet physiological needs such as warmth and comfort, and psychological needs such as improved self-esteem or status. There are the obvious tangible elements to a garment including fabric (handle, weight and texture), fit, trims, embellishment, colour, quality of manufacture, brand name, sizing and price. Non-tangible elements such as image, identification with a peer group, status, aspirations, credibility, exclusivity, style and more practical elements such as comfort and washability can have even more influence on the customer's decision to purchase a garment.

The fashion buyer should take these non-tangible elements into account when developing products rather than focusing narrowly on the more tangible aspects of clothing. The importance of these factors in garment purchase can vary depending on customer type. A younger image-conscious customer is probably more influenced by credibility and peer-group acceptance than an older customer who may prioritise practical considerations instead. The same customer may place importance on different factors depending on the purpose of the garments; a woman in middle management may spend most of her clothing budget on clothes for work where her status and career aspirations are reflected in her choice of outfits, and she may spend less on leisurewear for the weekend when practicality and comfort are important when she is spending time with her children.

Because customers do not change their whole wardrobes every season, changes to a garment range need to be incremental. The extent of change depends on the potential customer at whom the range is aimed and how quickly they respond to fashion trends. At the more innovative end of the market customers are looking for new merchandise at the introductory stage of the product life cycle, which will probably be worn with garments from previous seasons. It is a common perception that, in the womenswear and menswear markets, the younger the customers the more receptive they are to innovation. As discussed earlier, this is not always the case, as lifestyle and disposable income are often more influential on fashion purchases than age. Retailers can organise consumer panels which meet periodically to give feedback on certain aspects of stores or products, and buyers may occasionally be invited to participate in or listen to these discussions.

Summary

Fashion buyers have a great deal of influence in the marketing of a retailer's products. In the marketing mix buyers are instrumental in developing the product and finalising prices. Fashion styles have a finite product life cycle which may vary from a few weeks for a fad to many years for a classic item. Retailers define customer profiles to describe the demographics and life style of the consumer at whom the merchandise is aimed. Market research methods may be used to give buyers feedback on customers' opinions of the range. The customer's needs should be considered at all stages of the buying cycle.

References and further reading

Easey, M. (2002) *Fashion Marketing: Second Edition.* Blackwell Publishing, Oxford.

Hines, T. and Bruce, M. (2001) *Fashion Marketing: Contemporary Issues.* Butterworth Heinemann, Oxford.

Kotler, P., Wong, V., Saunders, J. and Armstrong, G. (2004) *Principles of Marketing: Fourth European Edition.* FT Prentice Hall, London.

Chapter 12

Careers in Fashion Buying

Just as the role of the buyer varies in each organisation, so do the promotional structures of buying departments and the qualifications and career path of each buyer. It is possible for a buyer with a BA (Hons) fashion degree to work alongside another buyer who is a history graduate, and both of them may work for a senior buyer with no post-A-level qualifications. The non-graduate senior buyer is likely to have had retail experience, or to have started work at the company as an administrator picking up skills on the job, both of which may have taken longer than a degree. When employing buyers, stores may value enthusiasm more highly than a fashion degree.

Having a relevant higher education qualification is not vital for a buyer but it is becoming increasingly important in a competitive retail environment. Most graduates with design-related degrees may initally expect to become designers, but according to the fashion recruitment specialist Vanessa Denza MBE, the majority are more likely to be employed in other roles within the industry. Students are becoming aware of the central role played by buyers in the development of fashion products to the extent that it is an increasingly popular alternative career option to fashion design. According to a survey of 17 UK higher education institutions by the British Fashion Council most fashion students graduating in 1999 were employed in roles other than designers, with fashion buying being second only to fashion design as an employment outlet.

Buyers often travel more and can earn more money than designers and this makes fashion buying a tempting career path for many graduates. Most fashion designers are employed by clothing manufacturers and, with the gradual demise of UK garment production since the 1980s, much production has moved overseas. However, retailers have remained in their home countries maintaining a consistent demand for buyers, many of whom are expected to initiate product designs when dealing with offshore manufacturers without design facilities. Staff turnover within the fashion industry can be relatively high in comparison with other types of business and many buyers change jobs every two to three years. There are various reasons for this, including better employment packages or prospects, being head-hunted, redundancy and internal politics, but boredom is very seldom one of the reasons.

Is fashion buying the right career for you?

Ask yourself whether you are the right type of person to undertake a career in fashion buying. Do not be lured by the potential financial and travel incentives if you are not prepared for the hard work which accompanies these perks. Many of the skills listed in this book can be learned in the workplace but others, such as communication skills, depend heavily on personality. Researching into fashion buying, by talking to buyers for example, is useful but you cannot know for certain whether or not you are going to make it until you work in a fashion buying department. Even then, if you find you do not like the job it may be because of the way that your particular department operates at that time or the way in which your line manager works, rather than because buying is unsuitable for you. Do not be surprised if you are expected to work long hours even at assistant buyer level as this is the norm in many buying departments. Buyers usually have to work weekends when necessary, during an overseas trip or before a key departmental meeting.

It is possible to request a transfer to another department as many retailers offer a flexible career path with sideways moves, such as from womenswear to menswear buying. If you have established a good reputation your employer may prefer to keep you in the company by offering an alternative job rather than losing you to another retailer. Most employers expect their buyers to be adaptable with the flexibility to move to new product areas, and you may be asked to take on a different area without requesting to be moved if your skills are required elsewhere.

Qualifications for a career in fashion buying

There are many different routes into a career as a fashion buyer as shown by the case studies in this book, but probably the most typical route into fashion buying after GCSEs would be to take A levels (at least one in an art and design subject) and a one-year foundation course. A shorter route taken by many buyers is to gain a BTEC National Diploma in fashion (or general art and design) at a further education or art college. After a foundation or National Diploma course the next stage is to enrol on a relevant degree course such as a BA (Hons) Fashion Design degree or an associated subject such as fashion marketing. A degree takes at least three years to complete. Many degree courses expect applicants to have gained at least five GCSEs at grade C or above (though some accept a minimum of three), and BTEC National Diploma courses usually require four or more. However, in both further and higher education, 'exceptional entry' students may be admitted with less than the minimum requirements, if they have a particularly strong portfolio of project work or experience in industry or are mature students. Some universities offer a four-year sandwich course which includes up to a year working in the fashion industry. This extra year is extremely valuable as it gives the undergraduate some experience of how the industry operates in practice.

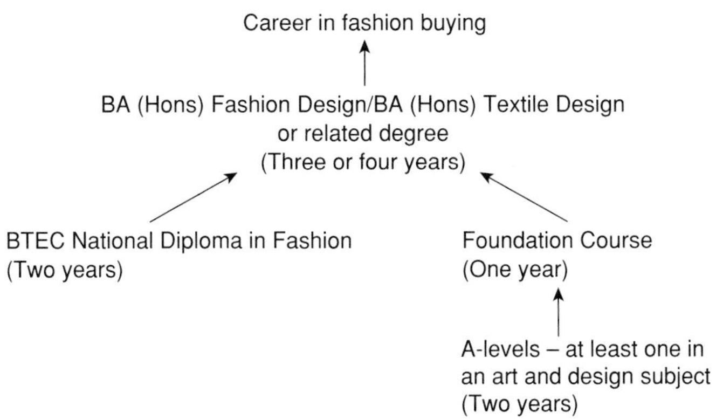

Figure 12.1 Possible routes into fashion buying after completion of GCSEs.

As discussed above and shown in Figure 12.1 there are many buyers who are exceptions to the above routes in terms of education, though, with an increasing number of students graduating from design courses in the UK, it is anticipated that in future a higher proportion of fashion buyers will possess a fashion degree. Several BA (Hons) courses in fashion marketing, product development or fashion promotion have been launched with the aim of producing graduates to work within the fashion business in roles other than design, including buying. Many buyers are graduates in closely related fields such as textiles, or in diverse subjects such as business studies or English. If you are currently looking for an appropriate degree course to prepare you for a career in buying check the university's prospectus to see whether buying is addressed within the curriculum, as this is likely to be considered an advantage by employers. Sometimes employees from different departments within fashion retailers, sales managers, head office administrative staff or merchandisers progress into buying. Sales staff can bring with them a wealth of valuable knowledge about the company's customers which may be considered equivalent to a higher education qualification. A graduate who has years of experience in working part-time on the sales floor whilst studying for a degree has a distinct advantage for many employers looking for trainee buyers.

Relevant skills for fashion buyers

To achieve a successful career in buying, you will require:

- qualifications or relevant experience
- effective interpersonal and communication skills
- decision-making, analytical and numeracy skills
- enthusiasm for your job
- knowledge of the relevant fashion market (product, customers and competitors).

Though qualifications and experience are not the only factors which retailers consider when employing buyers, they are the main elements which make one CV stand out from the rest. You may have ideal personal qualities for a career as a buyer but obviously these are unlikely to be noticed unless you manage to get an interview for the job. Gaining fashion retail experience and/or a relevant qualification will therefore give you a stronger chance of being employed in a buying department. If you are suitably qualified, retail experience in a different field from fashion may also be useful in helping you to get an interview. Even if you spent three years working in a restaurant whilst studying for your degree, you can stress the transferable skills which you utilised, such as communication, teamwork and organisation. However, working in a fashion store is the part-time job which most retailers or job agencies would hope to see on a CV from a student who is about to graduate and is applying for a fashion buying post. Many students need to work to support themselves but even if you can afford to pay your own way through college it is worth working simply to enhance your employability after graduation. If you have a choice of jobs, you should aim to work for a fashion retailer with a high profile such as a store selling designer brands, or an innovative mass market retailer, which is likely to impress a more mainstream retailer. The experience which you gain by meeting consumers directly will be invaluable in assisting you to make effective buying decisions. Most retailers send their buyers on store visits regularly, sometimes in the role of shop assistants working in the changing rooms, to give them a first-hand and therefore realistic perspective on the customer.

Career progression in fashion buying

Buying positions in companies vary in terms of responsibilities and pay – a buying manager working for one retailer may have an equivalent role and salary to a senior buyer for a different store. Smaller companies tend to have more of a flat management structure, with perhaps an assistant buyer progressing directly to buyer. An example of a typical career progression route is shown in Figure 12.2 (see also case studies of Jaeger and Oasis in Chapter 8). Some larger companies may also operate in this way to reduce layers of

Figure 12.2 Typical career progression route in fashion buying.

management. Many large retailers employ buyer's assistants or buyer's administrators (at a junior level to the trainee buyer). Some graduates may consider applying for such positions as a route into a buying career, but the work tends to be mainly administrative and less responsible than the assistant buyer's role.

Methods of finding jobs in fashion buying

Finding your first job in fashion buying can be a demanding task and it is important to keep trying, expect some rejection letters and see any interview opportunities as valuable experience. Remember that if you are called for an interview it means that someone considers that your experience and qualifications are suitable for a job. If you are not offered the position, it may simply be that your competitors were more suitably qualified. If you do not get a particular job it is worth contacting the employer's human resources (HR) or personnel department to ask whether you could have improved on any aspects. You must ask this in a positive and non-challenging way if you are to get a response. You must also realise that they are very busy and may not have time to reply to you. The fashion recruitment expert Vanessa Denza recommends contacting the company if you do not hear from them after applying for a job:

> If you receive no response from a cover letter and CV or application form, phone or write a follow-up letter. Do not call the receptionist every day. Avoid making judgements as to why you have not heard back. Be persistent but not overly so. If they don't call you, don't assume they are not interested.

Fashion buying recruitment usually takes place by the following methods:

- press advertising: fashion trade press, national and local newspapers
- writing speculative letters to employers
- word of mouth
- internal vacancies
- fashion employment agencies.

Press advertising

Fashion trade magazines, such as *Drapers* in the UK, have specialised sections for appointments which usually run to several pages. Employers often advertise vacancies themselves and even if a current vacancy is not suitable it is worth making a note of a retailer's head office address and a name from the HR department for future reference. You should consider subscribing to a trade magazine if you are looking for a job as it is important to respond quickly to advertisements. National newspapers are usually used only for senior positions or large-scale graduate recruitment as advertising space is relatively expensive. The local press can be a good source of vacancies in the major clothing industry regions such as London, the east Midlands and North-West. If you do not live in these areas but would be willing to relocate it is worth either buying the local newspapers by mail order or visiting to look at advertisements in the local press.

Word of mouth and internal advertising

Press advertising is the most obvious recruitment method to use, but word of mouth is an extremely popular alternative and most buyers are likely to be recruited in this way at some point in their careers. A buyer could hear about a post in another company from a friend who works there and apply before the position is advertised, or a buyer could be approached directly by another retailer who has heard of the buyer by reputation. Garment suppliers can sometimes act as go-betweens in this situation as they usually work with more than one retailer and are ideally placed to be able to recommend appropriate buyers. When a vacancy arises the company may prefer to recruit internally by identifying suitable candidates for promotion. Some retailers issue their own internal vacancy bulletins so existing employees can be offered opportunities first before the company takes the more expensive route of advertising externally.

Fashion recruitment agencies

Several recruitment agencies specialise solely in the fashion industry. Some concentrate on particular segments of the industry, such as buying, design or graduate recruitment. Most of the UK fashion recruitment agencies are based in London including Denza International who recruit for the fashion industry at all levels including graduates for posts in the UK and overseas. There are also fashion recruitment agencies located outside London such as the Ross Group in Manchester and People Marketing in Nottingham. The agencies often advertise in *Drapers* listing numerous vacancies, usually with a brief job title, location and salary. The employers in such advertisements maintain their anonymity, mainly so that other agencies do not approach them directly, and fashion companies with a high turnover of staff may not want this to be publicised. The employment agencies charge the employers rather than the applicants for their services as a company is more likely to be able to afford to pay for this than an individual searching for a job. The agencies are usually paid on results so their recruitment consultants are strongly motivated to match applicants to jobs. Deals between recruitment agencies and employers are confidential and usually involve the agency being paid a percentage of the employee's annual salary by the employer if the individual remains in the job for at least an agreed length of time. The employee is not usually party to the details of this agreement.

Agencies mostly prefer to interview people who apply to them, either in person or by telephone, before putting them forward for a job. This is so that they can make their own assessment of the applicant in an informal interview and can discuss their skills and job requirements. Once you are on the books of a fashion recruitment agency you will be contacted when a suitable vacancy arises and the agency will forward your details to the company if you are interested in the position. It is worth registering with several agencies when seeking a buying job. Many of the agencies focus on jobs that require three years experience or more, some at executive level only, but others specialise in junior positions for graduates. Some agencies use head-hunting tactics to find the right person for a job by directly approaching a buyer with the right experience. Buyers may be approached in this way even though they are not intending to change jobs, either because someone has recommended them or because they hold a similar position within a competing retailer. This can reduce the workload of a recruitment consultant by targeting only candidates compatible with the job on offer rather than searching through many often inappropriate CVs. Some agencies ring retailers' head offices to ask the name of the buyer of a particular product area for which they are recruiting, and receptionists are often not permitted to give out buyers' names in case their staff are being approached in this way. The internet has substantially improved the recruitment process as fashion recruitment agencies' websites are updated frequently and the pool of potential job candidates has been widened. www.retailchoice.com allows applicants access to buying and other retail positions from numerous recruitment agencies. Certain websites specialise in finding recruitment for fashion graduates, allowing them the opportunity to exhibit their work to an international audience.

Writing speculative letters to retailers

It is possible to find a job by writing speculative letters to companies for whom you would like to work. This can be rather time-consuming, but it is possible to find work this way and can be worth the time and effort. Employers can find this useful as being approached by suitable candidates can save them time and money thereby avoiding the need to advertise. Think about which retailers you would like to target and find out where they are located. It is advisable to write to the HR department, as they should be aware of all current and imminent vacancies. If your CV and letter show that you have the skills required by the retailer you may even be interviewed before a vacancy arises, particularly if you are an experienced buyer. You can find head office addresses by looking in *Yellow Pages*, visiting the company's website or reading relevant publications. Another effective method of finding this information is to ask shop assistants in the store's branches; they can be very helpful and may even have a list of staff in the company's buying department to whom you could write. You can also write a speculative letter to an agency enclosing your CV even if they are not currently advertising a suitable post.

CVs

Your CV should be clearly legible and well presented on a maximum of two A4 pages. The first page needs to be interesting enough to hold the employer's attention and make them want to read further. Consider adapting your CV to suit the job or company for which you are applying, so if the post is for menswear put your menswear project from college at the top of the list of course content. This extra bit of effort could potentially be the deciding factor in gaining an interview. You should begin with factual details including your name, address, date of birth and telephone number/email address. Your employment and education details should then be listed in reverse chronological order with the start and finish dates. If you are a graduate ensure that you give a summary of some of the relevant subjects studied on your course as well as the course title and educational institution, as employers are unlikely to be familiar with the course content. Mention the grades of your qualifications only if they are particularly good (As or Bs and first class or upper second class degrees). List any jobs you have had in the fashion industry including placements and part-time employment, briefly mentioning your responsibilities and some of the main elements that you learned from each job. Add any additional skills or abilities at the end of your CV. Employers may be interested in your computer skills, particularly on CAD or word-processing programs, as well as languages.

Interview structure

Many interviews for buyers involve panels of interviewers. This usually includes the line manager for the post who may be a buyer or buying manager and at least one other member of staff, such as a buyer from another product area or a member of the human resources (personnel) department. There are likely to be at least two interview stages with the best candidates from the initial interviews being invited back for a second interview, probably with some different members on the panel. Some of the larger retailers ask applicants who have recently graduated to undertake an aptitude test before they are invited for interview. This may be sent to them by post or take place at the head office, testing written skills, numeracy and product knowledge. Many retailers use psychometric tests before interview stage, where there are no right or wrong answers, but the results can help to indicate a profile of the candidates' interpersonal skills. Some retailers invite graduates to participate in recruitment days that include a range of relevant activities. This enables the company to observe how individuals perform in practice and allows candidates to demonstrate their interpersonal skills with the emphasis on working well within a team to solve a set task.

Advice for interviewees

You may have the ideal skills to enable you to be a successful buyer but you will obviously not have the chance to implement them unless you perform well enough in an interview to be offered a job. Interviewers for fashion buying positions are often surprised by interviewees' lack of preparation, particularly with regard to research into the company. You need to convince the interviewer that you are very interested in working for the company by doing your homework beforehand. Another surprise for interviewers is that some candidates applying for a buying position for the first time have no idea what being a buyer involves. Applicants should expect to be asked this question at an interview, and prepare for it accordingly. By reading this book you will have become familiar with the tasks that take place within a buying department and you should be prepared to demonstrate that you have some knowledge of buying during the interview. Motivation is one of the key skills required for buyers and, as it is not always possible to show this through qualifications or experience, your enthusiasm during the interview, as well as the amount of relevant research which you have done beforehand, will indicate to the employer how well-motivated you are. Your aim in an interview situation should be to project confidence and competence without appearing to be arrogant.

It is not necessary to rely entirely on your natural ability at interviews as there are many ways in which you can plan to increase your chances of getting the job you want. Remember that many managers have not received any training in interviewing people so if you have learnt how to be a good interviewee you could have an advantage over the interviewer. The following list suggests a variety of ways in which you can improve your interview skills by careful planning. You may find it difficult to remember all of these suggestions, but if you apply just a few of them it may help you to clinch the job.

- Present yourself appropriately.
- Find out as much as you can about the company first, though you will not be expected to know everything. Look at stores, customers, websites, articles about the company and annual reports.
- Anticipate which questions you will be asked and plan appropriate answers. Practise your responses with a friend, if possible.
- Keep up-to-date on trends in the industry – read trade magazines.
- Think about which skills and abilities the employer will be looking for.
- Read your application form and CV again before the interview, to remind yourself what you have written.
- Remind yourself of appropriate questions before the interview.
- Think positively. You only get an interview if it looks like you could probably do the job. You have already been short-listed.

Presentation at interviews

Presenting yourself appropriately is obviously essential in the fashion industry. If your clothing is a little too over-the-top this may be interpreted by the interviewer as suggesting that you are more interested in becoming a designer and that buying is therefore a second choice or compromise. Conversely if your clothes are viewed as out-of-date or too serious this may imply to the interviewer that you are not particularly interested in fashion. You need to show through your choice of clothes that you are aware of fashion, but with a touch of formality that reflects a business-like and well-organised approach. This does not necessarily mean wearing a suit, but an over-casual outfit should be avoided. What you should wear for an interview obviously varies depending on current trends and it is advisable to choose an outfit which includes the must-have item for the season in the latest colour. This is literally a case of investment dressing, as your appearance could be one amongst several factors which help to get you the job. If you can afford it aim to buy your outfit from a store which is more fashionable and in a slightly higher price bracket than the company which has offered you an interview. (If you cannot afford it may be worthwhile trying to borrow the money for an outfit, knowing that your investment will pay off if you land the right job.) Take care in choosing your accessories, make-up and hairstyle for the interview, giving yourself a total look with the aim of impressing, but not shocking, the interviewer.

Advice during the interview

- First impressions and last impressions are very important.
- Be polite to all members of staff, not just the interviewer.
- Remember that effective communication means listening as well as talking.
- Ask informed questions about the company.
- Do not argue.
- Tell the truth – be honest, but selective in what you say.
- Do not volunteer negative information about yourself.
- Use positive body language (non-verbal communication).
- Give examples to demonstrate your qualities and skills.
- Explain career gaps if necessary.
- Say 'I can' (not 'I think' or 'I feel').

First impressions

It has often been quoted that interviewers make up their minds about whether or not to offer a job within the first ten minutes of an interview and this is likely to be true in many cases. Research has shown that people tend to remember most clearly the first and last things that they are told, so you should consider the effect that this will have on an interviewer and ensure that your first and last comments make an impact. The first impression is crucial, but don't let this make you too apprehensive; if you make a mistake at the beginning of the interview just make sure you correct it as soon as you realise you have done it. Sometimes employers are just as nervous as applicants, particularly if the interviewer is inexperienced at interviewing. You should ensure that any contact you have with company personnel before the interview shows you in a positive light as you should expect them to inform the interviewer if you are perceived as a problem applicant. The HR department will not appreciate it should you complain vigorously at not receiving an application form immediately, and the receptionist will not be impressed if you behave rudely on your arrival. Bear in mind that the receptionist is possibly the only person who is familiar with every member of staff in the company, and has the opportunity to speak to them all on an almost daily basis.

Effective communication during an interview

An effective communicator usually aims to seek a balance by talking for an equal amount of time with the other participants in a conversation. As an interviewee you will probably be expected to speak for more than half of the time as the focus is largely on you and your suitability for the job. You also need to listen attentively and carefully to the interviewer/s. How you present yourself is as much about how you communicate as how you dress. Your careful choice of outfit should help to boost your confidence, enabling you to relax a little. Consider your non-verbal communication (NVC), such as body language, during the interview, as this can say as much about you as your verbal skills. If you perch uncomfortably on the edge of the chair or have your arms tightly folded in front of you throughout the interview you will appear nervous and defensive. Try to achieve an open and relaxed approach, without coming across as too laid-back. Practise this by sitting down in front of a mirror, or asking a friend to observe your posture, and alter your position if you do not appear to be at ease. Smile occasionally if relevant (though not too much or it may appear that you are not taking the interview seriously). Make sure you maintain eye contact during the interview, and you should aim to look at each member of a panel of interviewers in turn. Focusing on one person can be a mistake, as you may have identified the wrong person as the key member of the panel and that key person may not be the one who asks the most questions.

Ask relevant questions about the company but don't expect confidential information to be revealed to you. It is acceptable to ask whether they sell more of one product type than another, but they are unlikely to give you very specific details such as the current bestseller in the range. It is possible for you to engage in a little debate on a subject within the interview but it is obviously not advisable to be argumentative, however strongly you feel about the topic. You need to be honest in an interview, particularly when asked direct questions, as the fashion business has its own grapevine, and you should expect to be found out if you lie about something, for instance if you were to say that you resigned from a certain job when you were actually made redundant. However you need to be selective in your comments and avoid advertising any negative points about yourself, so don't mention your weaknesses unless asked. Some interviewers will ask you to explain your strengths and weaknesses, so be prepared for this question. When planning your response, make sure that the list of your strengths is the longest. Ensure that amongst your strengths are relevant qualities and skills for the job and give examples as evidence. Consider your weaknesses and try to phrase them in a positive way so that they appear to be redeemable; 'my computer skills are average, but I want to improve, so I've registered for a nightclass'. During the interview, aim to use assertive and confident phrases such as 'I can' or 'I will', rather than being vague.

Questions to ask at interviews

Remember that the interview is a two-way process. It is important for the company to find out whether you are the right person for the job and you need to know whether the job will be right for you. Interviewers usually ask if you have any questions, often at the close of the interview, and you could prepare for this by asking some of the questions below. Do not ask all of these questions, but select two or three and prioritise them. If you only ask about the salary, holidays and travel, you could give the impression that they are the motivation behind your application. Although this may be partly true, it would be a good idea not to make it so obvious to the interviewers. You should also prepare one or two questions that are directly relevant to the job for which you have applied. Make sure you have listened carefully to their comments in the interview, as some of the questions you have prepared could have been answered earlier. Try not to look shocked at their responses: if the interviewer says that buyers often work until 7 p.m., don't ask whether overtime is paid as the answer will invariably be 'no'. You may wish to select two or three relevant questions from the following list to ask during an interview for a buying post:

- Are you conducting second interviews for this job?
- When will I hear from you about the job?
- What opportunities are there for promotion and progression in this post?
- How many days of annual leave would I have?
- What are the regular working hours?
- Does the job include any travel? (If so, where and when?)
- Would I be based at head office?
- What salary are you offering for this post? (Consider asking this at the end of the interview.)

After the interview

You usually cannot tell whether or not you have got a job depending on how well you feel the interview went. Sometimes people are offered jobs when they are convinced that the interview went badly and others are surprised to be rejected after a seemingly positive interview. This is mainly because employers have a wide range of approaches to interviewing and many interviewers purposely take a tough approach to see how the applicant copes under pressure. If you should be offered a post, consider carefully before you accept it. If this is your first job it is a decision that could define the rest of your career. If you can manage financially, don't necessarily take the first job you are offered if you do not feel comfortable about it. If necessary, seek advice from your lecturers, family and friends before accepting a post, but the final decision must rest with you.

Summary

Many fashion buyers have fashion-related degrees, although it is not essential to have studied fashion to take up a career in buying. Buyers need to have a strong interest in fashion, combined with interpersonal skills such as teamwork and time management. Fashion buying jobs can be found mostly through advertisements in the trade press, word of mouth and fashion recruitment agencies. Knowledge of the retailer to whom the candidate has applied for a job, an awareness of the buyer's role, and careful planning can be advantageous when being interviewed for a buying position.

Further reading

Goworek, H. (2006) *Careers in Fashion and Textiles.* Blackwell Publishing, Oxford.
Middleton, J. (2005) *High Impact CVs.* Infinite Ideas, Oxford.

Websites

www.denza.co.uk
www.inretail.co.uk
www.peoplemarketing.co.uk
www.prospects.ac.uk
www.retailchoice.com
www.work-experience.org

Glossary of Fashion Buying Terms

Allocators are responsible for allocating specific styles and quantities of merchandise to retail outlets. (Some retailers refer to this role as branch merchandiser or optimiser.)

Art directors are responsible for designing the layout of a brochure or mail order catalogue, including the coordination of photo shoots.

Branded merchandise refers to products which have not been designed or developed in-house by the retailer, and are sold under the brand name of the supplier. This applies mainly to middle-market and designer-level products.

CIF stands for 'carriage, insurance and freight'. It applies to the price charged for a product by a supplier, meaning that the product's price includes delivery and insurance for the goods from the supplier's premises to a specified location (such as a UK port). It is often used with reference to the price per metre of a fabric.

Classics are products which have a long-term appeal to consumers, usually for a period of years.

CMT stands for 'cut, make and trim'. This term is applied to garment manufacturers who do not provide design or pattern cutting facilities, and are purely involved in the cutting and manufacturing processes.

Colour palette refers to a selected group of colours used within a coordinating range of products.

Colourway is the term for a colour in which a particular garment is produced. Many fashion garments are sold in more than one colourway to offer the customer a wider choice, thereby maximising sales. Several garments within a coordinated range may be produced in the same colourway.

Comparative shopping is research into comparable products available from competing retailers. Buyers and designers usually undertake comparative shopping at least once per season, either for their own reference or to produce reports to share with their colleagues.

Confined prints are fabric prints which are exclusive to a certain retailer for a given period of time.

Cost price is the price charged by a supplier to a retailer for a product.

Copywriters write the product descriptions used in mail order catalogues.

Core product refers to basic garment styles which are available for more than one season. (This term is interchangeable with **classic** product.)

Couture fashion is featured in catwalk shows, designed by couturiers based in Paris. Couture is the most expensive category of fashion merchandise, as it is individually fitted to each customer and garments are hand-sewn.

Critical path is the series of key deadlines for product development and production which must be met in order for a product range to be delivered to stores for a set date.

CSR stands for 'corporate and social responsibility'. Many retailers have developed CSR policies and some have employees to implement these policies in relation to sourcing products ethically.

Customer profile is a visual and/or written description of the type of customer at whom a retailer aims its products.

Diffusion ranges are garments produced by ready-to-wear designers at a cheaper price level than their standard ranges.

Directional shopping refers to trips for fashion designers and buyers to major fashion cities to provide inspiration and fashion concepts for future seasons.

Entry prices are the lowest retail price points within a range of products.

ETI stands for 'Ethical Trading Initiative', a collaboration between companies, non-governmental organisations (NGOs) and trade unions which aims to improve working conditions for employees of suppliers to the UK market.

Fabric merchants buy fabric in bulk, enabling them to sell it from stock, in lower quantities than the fabric manufacturer's minimum.

Fabric sourcing refers to the process of contacting fabric suppliers to select fabrics for garment ranges. Buyers, designers and fabric technologists can all be involved in fabric sourcing, which takes place mostly in meetings with sales representatives from fabric suppliers, or at fabric trade fairs.

Fabric technologists are responsible for ensuring that fabrics meet the quality standards required by fashion retailers. Fabric technologists can be employed by retailers, garment manufacturers or independent testing laboratories.

Fads are fashions which are popular for a relatively short period of time, usually no longer than one season.

Final range selection is the meeting at which buyers present samples of their ranges for a particular season to colleagues and management. This is usually the stage at which the range is finalised.

FOB stands for 'free on board'. The term applies to the price charged for a product by a supplier, meaning that the price does not include delivery and insurance for the goods. It is often used with reference to the price per metre of a fabric. The purchaser therefore has to arrange delivery of the goods, or pay an additional charge for the supplier to deliver them.

Garment sourcing refers to liaison between fashion retailers and garment suppliers, with the aim of selecting garments to be sold in retailers' product ranges.

Grades are samples of garment styles in a specified range of sizes, e.g. for womenswear this may include the standard size 12 as well as samples in the smallest and largest sizes which have been ordered.

Lab dye or 'lab dip' is a small swatch of a fabric selected for a garment style, dyed to a specified shade. Lab dyes are usually sent by fabric suppliers to buyers for approval before the fabric is dyed in bulk production.

Lead time is the total duration of time which elapses from placing an order to the delivery of goods. This usually includes production and transportation of the goods.

Mark-up is the difference between the cost price and retail selling price of a product.

Margin is another term for mark-up, and is usually expressed as a percentage of the selling price.

Merchandisers are responsible for ensuring that the products within a range are delivered from suppliers to the retailer in the right quantities at the right time. They work closely with buyers and suppliers to monitor the sales of current ranges and progress of ranges under development. (Merchandisers may be referred to as stock controllers in some companies.)

Minimums are the smallest amounts of products which suppliers can manufacture. It is rarely viable for the suppliers to make less than the specified minimum quantity of a product, due to the costs involved in developing products, unless a premium price is charged.

New line sheets are forms compiled by buyers and merchandisers listing all of the relevant details about an individual product style. The new line sheet is used by the retailer and supplier as the definitive reference document for the style. (Certain retailers have different terms for new line sheets, e.g. purchase orders.)

Open-to-buy is part of the retailer's budget for buying stock, retained for purchases close to or during a particular season, after the majority of the range has been bought.

Overseas sourcing offices are used by fashion retailers to liaise with suppliers in other countries.

Phases are periods within a season during which new merchandise is introduced to stores. Many fashion retailers develop ranges for at least three phases per season.

Point-of-sale refers to in-store promotional material, e.g. brochures and postcards.

Potential customers are those at whom a retailer aims its products, usually defined by age, life style and income bracket.

Pre-selection is a meeting prior to final range selection, at which buyers, merchandisers and QCs analyse a product range, making amendments to styles and prices where necessary.

Progress chasing involves checking the development of the products within a range, at each stage of the critical path, through liaison between buyers, suppliers, QCs and merchandisers.

PR stands for 'public relations'. Retailers use in-house PR departments or independent PR companies to contact the press to gain editorial coverage of the company's products in magazines and newspapers.

Product life cycle refers to the timescale from the launch of a product through to its decline.

QC stands for 'quality controller', or 'quality control'. Most fashion retailers employ QCs to monitor the quality standards of merchandise, and to ensure that products fit correctly. (Certain retailers refer to this role as QA (quality assurer) or garment technologist.)

Range plan is a chart containing the finalised details of each product within a range for a particular season.

Range planning involves planning the number and types of products required within a range for a future season, taking into account predicted fashion trends and historical sales information.

Ready-to-wear (also known by the French term *prêt-à-porter*) refers to garments by designers who show their ranges at the seasonal catwalk collections in cities such as London, Paris, Milan or New York. Ready-to-wear ranges are less expensive than couture ranges, as they are not made to fit individual customers, but cost substantially more than mass market garments.

Repeat orders are made by buyers or merchandisers for styles which are expected to sell out within a relatively short time. If the original supplier does not have sufficient production capacity, the buyer may place the repeat with another manufacturer if the design has been developed by the retailer, a process known as 'copy action'.

Sealing samples are samples of garments selected for a range, which have been finalised and approved for fit. The retailer's QC approves the style by signing a seal which is attached to the garment. Both the retailer and manufacturer retain a sealing sample for each style, to specify the standard which garments must achieve in production.

Spec. sheet is an abbreviation of 'specification sheet'. A spec. sheet is produced by a designer, containing a working drawing and details on garment make-up, fabric and trims, to enable a sample garment to be made.

Strike-off is the term used for the printing of a design onto a sample of fabric. Strike-offs are submitted to buyers for approval of colour before fabric is printed in bulk production.

TYLY stands for 'this year/last year'. This term refers to the current financial performance of a product range in comparison to the previous year, e.g. the amount of sales turnover for the range during a particular week.

Visual merchandising is the layout and presentation of products within retail outlets.

Wearer trials are used to test the durability of garments when worn, before products are delivered to stores. Volunteers are asked to wear and wash the garments for a specified time and the results are analysed by the manufacturer or retailer.

Index